THE

ULTIMATE VACATION
RENTAL PLAYBOOK

Lynn Trifilo's Guide to Maximizing Your Investment

"The Ultimate Vacation Rental Playbook: Lynn Trifilo's Guide to Maximizing Your Investment," by Lynn Trifilo, with Eddie Coleman. ISBN 978-1-63868-218-9 (softcover).

This book is dedicated to the following:

My four amazing souls (my children) who have been my driving force and source of motivation. You have given me the strength to keep persevering and to strive for excellence in everything I do. Your steadfast and loving support have been my inspiration to work diligently and to never give up.

I would like to thank my respected clients who have entrusted me with the care of their vacation rental properties and homes. Your trust in me and your appreciation of my work have given me a great sense of achievement and pride. It is an honor to serve you, and I am grateful for the opportunity to be a part of your lives.

To everyone who has contributed to this book in one way or another, thank you from the bottom of my heart. Your support and encouragement have meant the world to me, and I am forever grateful.

Most of all, I would like to acknowledge my parents, who have instilled in me the values of a hard work ethic, dedication, and attention to detail. To never give up and know that I have the power and strength within. They taught me how to trust and know the power of God.
They have been my constants, my mentors, continually teaching me the importance of excellence in everything I do. I am blessed to have their unwavering love and support, and I owe them everything.
My Mother, has been a foundational and pivotal point to many teachings and successes of my life.

Dedicated and published
In my mom's memory.
Nancy Trifilo
~11/3/1948-1/23/2024~

INTRODUCTION

Welcome to a journey of discovery, a voyage through the realm of vacation rentals, where success and prosperity are within your grasp.

"The Ultimate Vacation Rental Playbook: Lynn Trifilo's Guide to Maximizing Your Investment" is a labor of love, crafted with the passion and dedication of an industry expert who has spent countless hours observing, learning, and perfecting the art of vacation rental staging, cleaning, and management.

As a distinguished expert consultant and owner of OCD Cleaning and Staging, LLC (Formally, OCD Cleaning Services Maui. LLC). Lynn Trifilo possesses a unique perspective on the industry. This vantage point has allowed her to identify the common pitfalls, overlooked opportunities, and hidden gems that can propel your vacation rental business to new heights.

This book aims to be a beacon of light for those seeking to navigate the often-murky waters of vacation rental ownership. It is our sincerest hope that the knowledge contained within these pages will serve as a catalyst for your own success, making your journey more predictable and enjoyable.

"The Ultimate Vacation Rental Playbook" is based on real-life experiences and the triumphs and tribulations of actual vacation rental owners and managers. It is a treasure trove of wisdom gleaned from years of observation and analysis, as well as Lynn's own experiences as an expert consultant.

This comprehensive guide offers you the opportunity to benefit from the expertise of a seasoned professional and to learn from the mistakes and successes of others in the industry.

As you delve into the chapters that follow, you will uncover invaluable insights, proven strategies, and powerful tactics to maximize your investment. Through Lynn's expert guidance, you will learn how to stage your property for the ultimate guest experience, maximize your rates, foster guest loyalty, and master the art of organic marketing.

You will also discover the secrets to success on platforms like VRBO and Airbnb and learn how to harness the power of referrals to grow your business.

Embrace the exciting world of vacation rentals, and let "The Ultimate Vacation Rental Playbook" illuminate your path to success. The journey ahead is one of limitless potential and prosperity. Happy reading, and may your vacation rental endeavors flourish!

Table of Contents:

ONE :
Embarking on the Vacation Rental Journey: A Profitable Adventure Awaits

Welcome to the exhilarating world of vacation rentals - a realm of opportunity, success, and rewards that await those who dare to take the plunge. As you embark on this journey, it's important to remember that you are not alone.

Countless others have walked this path before you, and with the right guidance and resources, you can transform your vacation rental dreams into a thriving reality.

In this chapter, we'll explore:

- The vast potential of the vacation rental market
- Essential steps to kick-start your journey
- Tips to build a strong foundation for success
- How to stay motivated and focused on your goals

The Potential of the
Vacation Rental Market

The vacation rental market is booming and for good reason. More and more travelers are seeking unique, personalized experiences that go beyond traditional hotel stays. This presents a golden opportunity for you to create memorable experiences for your guests while simultaneously building a profitable business.

Here's a glimpse of what awaits you in this thriving market:

- A growing number of travelers are choosing vacation rentals over hotels, providing a steady stream of potential guests.
- The opportunity to showcase your creativity in designing and staging your property to create a one-of-a-kind guest experience.
- A chance to capitalize on niche markets, such as eco-friendly stays, pet-friendly accommodations, or luxury retreats.
- The ability to build a business that reflects your passions and interests, while also generating income.

Kick-starting Your Journey

As you embark on your vacation rental journey, it's essential to start with a strong foundation. Here are some key steps to help you get started:

- Research your target market: Understand the preferences and expectations of your ideal guests to tailor your offerings accordingly.
- Choose the right property: Location, size, and amenities are all crucial factors to consider when selecting the perfect vacation rental property.
- Plan your budget: Be prepared for the initial investment and ongoing costs associated with running a successful vacation rental.
- Understand local regulations: Familiarize yourself with the rules and regulations governing vacation rentals in your area to ensure compliance and avoid potential issues.
- Network with other vacation rental owners: Connect with others in the industry to share experiences, tips, and resources.

Building a Strong Foundation for Success

To ensure the long-term success of your vacation rental business, it's crucial to build a strong foundation from the get-go. Here are some tips to help you lay the groundwork:

- Focus on exceptional guest experiences: Strive to exceed expectations in every aspect of your guest's stay, from the initial booking process to their departure.
- Prioritize cleanliness and maintenance: A spotless, well-maintained property is essential for attracting and retaining guests.
- Develop a solid marketing strategy: Utilize various marketing channels to showcase your property and reach your target audience.
- Implement systems and processes: Streamline your operations with efficient systems for bookings, communications, and maintenance.
- Stay adaptable: Be prepared to adjust your strategies and offerings based on market trends and guest feedback.

Staying Motivated and Focused

The vacation rental journey can be both exciting and challenging. To stay motivated and focused on your goals, consider the following:

- Set achievable milestones: Break your larger goals into smaller, attainable steps to maintain a sense of progress and accomplishment.
- Celebrate your wins: Acknowledge and celebrate your successes, both big and small, to maintain a positive mindset.
- Learn from your setbacks: Treat challenges as learning opportunities and use them to grow and improve your business.

- Stay connected to your "why": Regularly remind yourself of the reasons behind your vacation rental journey, whether it's financial freedom, creative expression, or the desire to provide exceptional experiences for your guests.

Navigating the World of Platforms and Channels

In the digital age, online platforms play a crucial role in connecting your property with potential guests. To maximize your reach, consider the following tips:

- Choose the right platforms: Evaluate popular vacation rentals websites such as Airbnb, VRBO, and Booking.com, and select the ones that align with your target audience and property type.
- Optimize your listings: Create compelling descriptions, use high-quality photos, and highlight the unique features of your property to stand out from the competition.
- Monitor your online reputation: Regularly track and respond to guest reviews to show your commitment to excellent customer service and to learn from valuable feedback.
- Utilize social media: Engage with potential guests and showcase your property through visually appealing content on platforms like Instagram, Facebook, and Pinterest.

Building a Memorable Brand

Creating a memorable brand for your vacation rental is vital in establishing a strong identity and setting yourself apart from the competition. Here's how you can build a brand that resonates with your target audience:

- Develop a unique value proposition: Identify the key elements that make your property stand out and use them to create a compelling narrative.
- Be consistent: Ensure that your branding, messaging, and overall guest experience are cohesive and consistent across all touchpoints.
- Connect with your audience: Foster genuine connections with your guests by sharing stories, experiences, and behind-the-scenes glimpses into your vacation rental journey.
- Encourage word-of-mouth marketing: Delighted guests are your best ambassadors. Provide exceptional experiences that inspire them to recommend your property to friends and family.

The Art of Pricing and Revenue Management

Pricing is a critical aspect of running a successful vacation rental business. To maximize your revenue, consider implementing the following strategies:

- Research the competition: Analyze the pricing trends of comparable properties in your area to determine a competitive rate.
- Employ dynamic pricing: Adjust your rates based on factors such as seasonality, local events, and booking patterns to capitalize on demand fluctuations.
- Offer value-added services: Enhance your guests' experience and generate additional revenue by offering services like airport transfers, meal plans, or personalized experiences.
- Monitor performance: Regularly review your booking data, occupancy rates, and revenue to identify opportunities for optimization and growth.

Conclusion: The Adventure Begins

As you embark on your vacation rental journey, remember that you hold the keys to unlocking a world of opportunity and success. With a strong foundation, a clear vision, and a commitment to excellence, you are well-equipped to turn your dreams into a thriving reality.

In the chapters ahead, you'll dive deeper into the intricacies of vacation rental management, exploring topics such as staging, guest loyalty, and online reviews. Each chapter is designed to provide you with actionable insights and strategies to elevate your vacation rental business to new heights.

So, buckle up and prepare for an exciting adventure filled with invaluable lessons, unforgettable experiences, and the satisfaction of seeing your investment flourish. The journey to vacation rental success begins now!

TWO:
Mastering the Art of Staging: Transform Ordinary Spaces into Extraordinary Places

In the competitive world of vacation rentals, it's not enough to merely offer a clean, comfortable space for your guests to rest their heads. To truly stand out from the crowd and create an unforgettable experience, you must master the art of staging—transforming ordinary spaces into extraordinary places that captivate and enchant your guests.

In this chapter, we'll explore the ins and outs of staging, equipping you with the tools and techniques to breathe life into your property and leave a lasting impression.

In this chapter, we'll cover:

- The importance of staging in the vacation rental industry
- Tips for selecting the perfect theme and style for your property
- How to create a functional, inviting layout
- The art of accessorizing: selecting the right decor and furnishings
- The role of lighting in setting the mood and ambiance

The Importance of Staging in the Vacation Rental Industry

Staging is a crucial element in the vacation rental experience, as it sets the stage for your guests' entire stay. A well-staged property can:

- Create a strong first impression: As soon as guests step into your property, they'll form an opinion based on its appearance. A beautifully staged space will instantly communicate that you care about their comfort and experience.
- Evoke positive emotions: A thoughtfully staged property can inspire feelings of relaxation, joy, and excitement, creating a lasting emotional connection with your guests.
- Increase bookings and revenue: A visually appealing property is more likely to catch the eye of potential guests, leading to increased bookings and, ultimately, higher revenue.
- Generate glowing reviews: Guests are more likely to leave positive reviews for properties that exceed their expectations, which in turn will attract even more guests.

Selecting the Perfect Theme and Style for Your Property

When it comes to staging your vacation rental, choosing the right theme and style is essential. To select the perfect look for your property, consider the following tips:

- Reflect the local culture and surroundings: Incorporate elements of the local environment, history, or culture to create a unique and authentic experience.
- Cater to your target audience: Keep in mind the preferences and expectations of your ideal guests when selecting a style. For example, if your property is geared toward families, opt for a fun, colorful theme with plenty of space for play and relaxation.
- Be true to your own taste: While it's important to cater to your guests, don't forget to infuse your own personality and preferences into your property's design.

Creating a Functional, Inviting Layout

A well-planned layout is key to ensuring your guests feel comfortable and at ease in your vacation rental. Here are some tips for designing a functional, inviting space:

- Maximize natural light: Arrange furniture and decor to allow for plenty of natural light, creating a bright, welcoming atmosphere.
- Create a comfortable atmosphere: Setting a comfortable temperature by staging the fans and air conditioners for the guests, upon their arrival, is welcoming.
- Ensure ample seating: Provide a variety of seating options, such as sofas, armchairs, and dining chairs, to accommodate different activities and group sizes.
- Prioritize functionality: Arrange furniture and amenities in a way that makes the most sense for your guests' needs, such as placing a coffee table near the seating area or a bedside table next to the bed.
- Create distinct areas: Use rugs, screens, or furniture arrangements to delineate separate spaces for different activities, such as relaxation, dining, or play.

The Art of Accessorizing: Selecting the Right Decor and Furnishings

The right decor and furnishings can make all the difference in creating a cohesive, stylish look for your vacation rental. Here are some tips for accessorizing your space:

- Choose a color scheme: Select a harmonious color palette to guide your choice of furnishings and decor, creating a visually appealing and cohesive space. Consider using neutral tones as a base, and adding pops of color with accent pieces, such as throw pillows or artwork.
- Incorporate texture: Mix and match different materials and textures, such as wood, metal, fabric, and glass, to create visual interest and depth in your space.
- Add personal touches: Display items with sentimental value, such as family heirlooms, travel souvenirs, or local artwork, to give your property a unique, personal feel.
- Avoid clutter: While it's important to create a warm, inviting atmosphere, be mindful not to overwhelm your space with too many items. Choose a few key pieces that complement your theme and style, and leave plenty of open space for guests to enjoy.

The Role of Lighting in Setting the Mood and Ambiance

Lighting is a powerful tool for creating a welcoming, comfortable atmosphere in your vacation rental. To make the most of your property's lighting, consider these tips:

- Layer your lighting: Use a combination of ambient, task, and accent lighting to create a versatile and adaptable space. For example, install dimmable overhead lights for general illumination, provide bedside lamps for reading, and highlight artwork with accent lights.
- Opt for warm tones: Warm-toned lighting creates a cozy, inviting atmosphere, making your guests feel more at ease. Choose bulbs with a warm color temperature (between 2700K and 3000K) for the best results.
- Consider smart lighting: Smart lighting systems, such as those that can be controlled via smartphone or voice commands, can add a touch of convenience and luxury to your guests' experience.
- Highlight outdoor spaces: Don't forget to illuminate outdoor areas, such as patios or balconies, with string lights or lanterns to create a cozy, inviting ambiance after the sun goes down.

Conclusion: Staging as a Key to Success

Mastering the art of staging is crucial in elevating your vacation rental business to new heights. By creating a visually stunning, functional, and inviting space, you can attract more bookings, garnering glowing reviews, and ultimately maximize your investment.

With a solid foundation in staging principles, you're now prepared to transform your property into an extraordinary haven that will delight and captivate your guests. In the next chapter, we'll delve into strategies for maximizing your rates and boosting your bottom line, ensuring that your hard work and dedication pay off in spades.

So, dear reader, let's continue our journey toward vacation rental success, as we explore the myriad ways to make your property shine brighter than the rest!

THREE:
Maximizing Your Rates: A Symphony of Strategies to Boost Your Bottom Line

In this chapter, we'll delve into the world of pricing strategies and financial planning, arming you with the knowledge and tools to maximize your rates and boost your bottom line. We'll start by exploring some unconventional tactics that can set your vacation rental apart from the competition, then dive deeper into the financial aspects of managing your property, drawing inspiration from the pages of the Harvard Business Review and other esteemed business texts. So, buckle up and get ready for an exhilarating ride into the realm of revenue optimization!

Unconventional Strategies to Set Your Property Apart

1. Offer unique experiences and amenities: Go beyond the standard offerings by providing exclusive experiences or amenities that cater to your target audience's interests and desires. For example, partner with a local chef to offer private cooking classes, or provide high-quality outdoor equipment for guests to use during their stay.
2. Dynamic pricing: Implement a dynamic pricing strategy that adjusts your rates based on factors such as seasonality, local events, and market demand. This approach ensures you're always charging the optimal rate for your property while remaining competitive in the market.
3. Target niche markets: Identify specific segments of travelers that align with your property's unique offerings and cater to their specific needs and preferences. This could include family-friendly accommodations, pet-friendly rentals, or properties tailored to adventure-seekers.
4. Create customizable packages: Offer tailored packages that allow guests to choose from a range of experiences and add-ons, enabling them to craft their ideal vacation. This not only increases the perceived value of your property but also allows you to charge a premium for these bespoke experiences.

Financial Planning and Management for Vacation Rental Success

1. Understand your costs: Develop a clear understanding of your property's fixed and variable costs, including mortgage payments, insurance, taxes, utilities, and maintenance expenses. This knowledge will help you make informed decisions about pricing and profit margins.

2. Set financial goals: Establish both short-term and long-term financial goals for your vacation rental business, such as annual revenue targets, occupancy rates, and desired return on investment. Having concrete objectives will help guide your pricing strategies and overall decision-making.

3. Conduct market research: Analyze your local market and competitor pricing to ensure your rates are competitive while still maximizing revenue. Stay up-to-date on industry trends and emerging technologies that could impact your business.

4. Implement revenue management techniques: Leverage revenue management principles, such as yield management and length-of-stay restrictions, to optimize your property's income potential. These techniques can help you maximize occupancy and revenue during peak seasons while minimizing vacancies during slower periods.

5. Track your performance: Regularly monitor your property's performance, comparing actual results to your financial goals and adjusting your strategies accordingly. This ongoing analysis will help you identify areas of improvement and capitalize on new opportunities.

6. Develop a contingency plan: Prepare for unexpected events or market shifts by developing a contingency plan that outlines steps to mitigate potential risks and safeguard your investment. This might include maintaining a reserve fund, securing additional financing options, or diversifying your marketing channels.

7. Continuously improve: Adopt a mindset of continuous improvement by regularly evaluating your property's performance, guest feedback, and market conditions. Implement necessary changes and enhancements to stay ahead of the competition and maximize your revenue potential.

Leveraging Technology and Data-Driven Decisions

1. Utilize pricing tools and software: Harness the power of technology by using pricing tools and software designed specifically for vacation rentals. These tools can help you analyze market trends, track your competitors, and optimize your pricing strategy based on real-time data.

2. Employ analytics: Dive deep into your property's performance data to identify trends, patterns, and areas for improvement. Analyze key performance indicators (KPIs) such as average daily rate (ADR), revenue per available room (RevPAR), and occupancy rate to make data-driven decisions that enhance your property's profitability.

3. Optimize your online presence: Ensure your property is visible and appealing to potential guests by optimizing your website and online listings. Use high-quality photos, engaging descriptions, and clear calls to action to entice visitors to book. Additionally, leverage search engine optimization (SEO) techniques to improve your property's visibility in search engine results.

4. Automate your operations: Streamline your vacation rental business by automating routine tasks, such as communication with guests, booking confirmations, and payment processing. By reducing manual efforts, you can focus on strategic initiatives that drive revenue growth and enhance your property's overall performance.

Building Strategic Partnerships and Alliances

1. Collaborate with local businesses: Forge partnerships with local businesses to provide exclusive offers and experiences for your guests. By creating a network of local partners, you can enhance your guests' vacation experience while promoting mutual growth within your community.
2. Engage with travel agencies and booking platforms: Establish relationships with travel agencies and online booking platforms to expand your reach and tap into new customer segments. By partnering with these intermediaries, you can access a broader audience and increase your property's visibility.
3. Participate in industry events and conferences: Attend vacation rental industry events and conferences to stay informed about the latest trends, technologies, and best practices. Networking with industry peers can also help you uncover new opportunities and partnerships that can drive your business forward.

Conclusion: Maximizing Rates for Long-Term Success

By embracing unconventional strategies, leveraging technology and data-driven decisions, and building strategic partnerships, you can effectively maximize your rates and boost your vacation rental's profitability. As you dive deeper into the world of financial planning and management, remember to stay agile and adapt your strategies to the ever-changing market conditions.

With a comprehensive understanding of the financial aspects of vacation rental management, you're well-equipped to navigate the complex landscape and drive long-term success for your property. In the next chapter, we'll explore the art of cultivating guest loyalty and rebooking rates, ensuring that your hard work translates into lasting relationships with your guests.

Ready for the next step in our journey? Let's continue to unlock the secrets of vacation rental success as we delve into the intricacies of guest loyalty and retention!

FOUR :
Cultivating Guest Loyalty:
How to Keep Them Coming Back for More

In this chapter, we'll dive into the fascinating world of customer loyalty and reveal the secrets to transforming your vacation rental guests into devoted fans who can't wait to return to your property.

Drawing on the wisdom of some of the greatest books on loyalty and customer devotion, we'll provide you with practical strategies and insights that can help you create a lasting bond with your guests and ensure their continued patronage.

So, let's embark on this exciting journey to unlock the true potential of guest loyalty in the vacation rental industry!

Understanding the Psychology of Loyalty

1. Emotional connection: Forge an emotional connection with your guests by providing an unforgettable experience that caters to their individual preferences and needs. Personalize their stay by remembering their likes and dislikes, and surprise them with thoughtful touches that demonstrate your genuine care.
2. Trust and reliability: Build trust with your guests by consistently delivering on your promises, ensuring a clean and well-maintained property, and providing seamless communication throughout their stay. When guests know they can rely on you, they're more likely to return.
3. Exceed expectations: Go above and beyond your guests' expectations by offering unique amenities, exceptional customer service, and delightful surprises. By consistently exceeding their expectations, you can create memorable experiences that foster lasting loyalty.

Strategies for Cultivating Guest Loyalty

1. Personalized communication: Engage in personalized communication with your guests before, during, and after their stay. This includes tailored email campaigns, timely text messages, and thoughtful follow-ups that show you care about their experience.
2. Loyalty programs and incentives: Establish a loyalty program that rewards guests for their repeat bookings, referrals, or even for sharing positive reviews. Offer incentives such as discounted rates

known as '*Kama'āina*' here on the islands, complimentary upgrades, or exclusive perks to keep them coming back for more.

3. Collect and act on feedback: Encourage guests to provide feedback about their stay, and actively use this information to improve your property and guest experience. By demonstrating that you value their opinions, you can foster a deeper sense of loyalty.

4. Foster a sense of community: Create a sense of belonging for your guests by engaging them through social media, newsletters, and other communication channels. Share news, updates, and stories about your property and local area to keep them connected and invested in your vacation rental.

Delivering Exceptional Customer Service

Anticipate your guests' needs: Be proactive in identifying your guests' needs and preferences. By anticipating what they might require or desire, you can provide them with a tailored experience that surpasses their expectations and keeps them coming back.

1. Be responsive and empathetic: Show genuine empathy and understanding when addressing your guests' concerns or complaints. Respond promptly and professionally, and always strive to find the best solution to ensure their satisfaction.

2. Empower your staff: Train and empower your staff to go above and beyond in providing exceptional customer service. Ensure they have the knowledge and resources to handle guest requests and issues confidently and effectively.

3. Continuous improvement: Continually evaluate and refine your customer service processes, policies, and training programs to ensure your team consistently delivers the highest level of service to your guests.

Creating Memorable Experiences

1. Offer unique and personalized experiences: Provide your guests with one-of-a-kind experiences tailored to their interests and preferences. This can include arranging local tours, offering exclusive amenities, or even partnering with local businesses to create bespoke packages.

2. Celebrate special occasions: Go the extra mile to make your guests feel special on their birthdays, anniversaries, or other important milestones. A small gesture, such as a complimentary cake or a personalized note, can make a big impact on their loyalty to your property.

3. Share insider tips and local secrets: Offer your guests insider information on the best local attractions, restaurants, and hidden gems in your area. By helping them explore the destination like a local, you can create a more authentic and memorable experience.

4. Embrace storytelling: Share captivating stories about your property, its history, and the local area to engage your guests on an emotional level. This can be done through your website, social media, or even in-person conversations during their stay.

Building Long-Lasting Relationships

1. Engage with guests post-stay: Maintain an open line of communication with your guests even after their stay. Send them personalized emails, holiday greetings, or exclusive offers to keep your property top-of-mind and encourage future bookings.
2. Leverage social media: Use social media platforms to engage with past, current, and potential guests. Share compelling content, ask for feedback, and respond to comments and messages to create a sense of community and connection with your audience.
3. Create a referral program: Encourage satisfied guests to spread the word about your property by offering incentives, such as discounts or special perks, for successful referrals. A well-designed referral program can help you tap into your guests' personal networks and generate more bookings.

Measuring and Monitoring Guest Loyalty

1. Track key performance indicators (KPIs): Monitor KPIs, such as repeat booking rate, guest satisfaction scores, and referral rates, to gauge the effectiveness of your guest loyalty initiatives. Analyzing these metrics can help you identify areas of improvement and adapt your strategies accordingly.
2. Conduct guest surveys: Regularly conduct guest surveys to gather valuable insights into your guests' preferences, expectations, and overall satisfaction. Use this feedback to fine-tune your offerings and enhance the guest experience.
3. Utilize customer relationship management (CRM) tools: Invest in CRM software to manage and analyze guest data effectively. CRM tools can help you better understand your guests' preferences, behaviors, and booking patterns, enabling you to create more targeted and personalized experiences.

The Importance of Genuine Care and Empathy

1. The author's personal experience: Her passion for the vacation rental industry was ignited by her own experiences as both a guest and an expert consultant. She understands the profound impact that genuine care, empathy, and personalized attention can have on a guest's overall experience, and she encourages property owners and managers to make these qualities the foundation of their approach to guest loyalty.
2. The power of human connection: In today's fast-paced, digital world, the value of genuine human connection cannot be overstated. By taking the time to truly understand your guests and their needs, you can create memorable experiences that resonate on a deeper, emotional level. Remember, when guests feel seen, heard, and valued, they are more likely to develop a strong sense of loyalty to your property.
3. The ripple effect of exceptional service: Providing exceptional service not only benefits your guests but can also create a positive ripple effect throughout your entire vacation rental operation. When guests become loyal advocates, they are more likely to spread the word about your property and attract even more satisfied guests. This, in turn, can lead to increased bookings, greater revenue, and a thriving business.

Embracing Continuous Growth and Improvement

1. Learning from your guests: Each guest interaction offers an opportunity to learn, grow, and improve your vacation rental business. By actively seeking feedback and applying the lessons you learn, you can continually refine your offerings and elevate the guest experience.

2. Adapting to the ever-changing landscape: The vacation rental industry is constantly evolving, and staying ahead of the curve requires a commitment to continuous growth and adaptation. By staying informed about industry trends, embracing new technologies, and remaining open to change, you can ensure that your property remains competitive and attractive to guests.

3. The pursuit of excellence: My personal philosophy is that the pursuit of excellence is a never-ending journey. She believes that by striving for constant improvement and embracing a growth mindset, vacation rental owners and managers can unlock their full potential and achieve unparalleled success in the industry.

The Art of Personalized Communication

1. My approach to communication: As an expert consultant in the vacation rental industry, I've always placed a strong emphasis on personalized communication. I believe that the key to creating long-lasting relationships with your guests is to make every interaction feel authentic and tailored to their unique needs.

2. Mastering the art of listening: One crucial aspect of personalized communication is truly listening to your guests. When you take the time to understand their preferences, concerns, and expectations, you're better equipped to deliver an experience that exceeds their expectations and strengthens their loyalty to your property.

3. Utilizing technology to enhance personalization: In today's digital age, there are numerous tools and platforms available that can help you streamline and personalize your communication with guests. From CRM software to automated messaging systems, these tools can enable you to maintain meaningful connections with your guests while saving time and resources.

The Power of Consistency and Reliability

1. Why consistency matters: In my years of experience in the industry, I've found that one of the most critical factors in building guest loyalty is consistently providing exceptional experiences. When guests know they can rely on your property for a memorable and hassle-free stay, they are more likely to return and recommend your property to others.

2. Creating consistent systems and processes: To ensure consistency across all aspects of your vacation rental operation, it's essential to develop and implement robust systems and processes. This includes everything from staff training and property maintenance to guest communication and feedback management.

3. Continually raising the bar: As you cultivate a culture of consistency and reliability, it's crucial not to become complacent. Always strive to raise the bar and seek ways to enhance the guest experience further. This commitment to continuous improvement will not only benefit your guests but also help you stay ahead of the competition and adapt to the ever-changing vacation rental landscape.

The Art of Surprise and Delight

1. My belief in the power of surprise: Over the years, I've witnessed firsthand the impact that unexpected surprises can have on a guest's experience. By going above and beyond to surprise and delight your guests, you can create lasting memories that keep them coming back for more.
2. Ideas for memorable surprises: There are countless ways to surprise and delight your guests, from offering personalized welcome gifts to arranging special experiences during their stay. The key is to tailor these surprises to your guests' preferences and interests, ensuring that each gesture feels thoughtful and unique.
3. The importance of timing: When it comes to delivering surprises, timing is crucial. Aim to surprise your guests at just the right moment – such as upon arrival, during a special occasion, or when they least expect it – to maximize the impact and create an unforgettable experience.

The Value of Trust and Transparency

1. Building trust with your guests: As a vacation rental owner and expert consultant, I've learned that trust is the foundation of any successful guest relationship. By being transparent, honest, and reliable in your interactions with guests, you can foster a sense of trust that leads to increased loyalty and repeat bookings.
2. Maintaining clear communication: One effective way to build trust with your guests is through clear and open communication. Be upfront about your property's policies, amenities, and any potential challenges, and address any questions or concerns promptly and honestly.
3. Embracing feedback and accountability: Another essential aspect of trust-building is being willing to accept feedback and take responsibility for any shortcomings in your guest's experience. By demonstrating a commitment to improvement and holding yourself accountable, you can strengthen your guests' trust in your property and your dedication to their satisfaction.

With these insights and strategies in mind, you'll be well-equipped to cultivate guest loyalty and ensure the continued success of your vacation rental business. Remember, the key to unlocking lasting loyalty lies in consistently providing exceptional experiences, building genuine connections, and constantly striving for growth and improvement.

The Role of Social Responsibility and Sustainability

1. My commitment to social responsibility: As an expert consultant in the vacation rental industry, I'm a firm believer in the importance of incorporating social responsibility and sustainability into your business practices. By doing so, you can not only improve the guest experience but also make a positive impact on the environment and the local community.
2. Sustainable practices to consider: There are numerous ways to incorporate sustainability into your vacation rental operation, such as using energy-efficient appliances, providing eco-friendly amenities, and implementing water-saving measures. These efforts can not only help protect the environment but also resonate with eco-conscious guests and set your property apart from the competition.
3. Supporting the local community: Another essential aspect of social responsibility is giving back to the local community. Consider partnering with local businesses, supporting community events, and

offering locally sourced products to your guests. These efforts can enhance the guest experience while also fostering a strong sense of community pride and connection.

Building a Strong Vacation Rental Brand

1. The importance of branding: In my years of experience, I've discovered that one of the most powerful ways to attract and retain loyal guests is by building a strong and recognizable brand for your vacation rental property. A well-crafted brand can communicate your property's unique value proposition and create an emotional connection with your guests.
2. Defining your brand identity: To create a compelling brand, start by defining your property's unique identity. Consider what sets your property apart from the competition, and what values and characteristics you want your guests to associate with your vacation rental experience.
3. Communicating your brand consistently: Once you've defined your brand identity, it's crucial to ensure that it is communicated consistently across all guest touchpoints. From your property's visual elements and decor to your marketing materials and guest interactions, make sure that every aspect of your vacation rental operation reflects your brand's core values and identity.

By incorporating these insights and strategies into your vacation rental business, you'll be well on your way to building a loyal guest base and achieving long-term success in the industry. Remember, the key to guest loyalty lies in consistently providing exceptional experiences, fostering genuine connections, and staying committed to growth and improvement.

The Importance of Online Presence and Reputation Management

1. My take on online presence: In today's digital world, having a strong online presence is vital for any vacation rental owner. As an expert consultant, I've witnessed the power of a well-crafted online presence in attracting and retaining guests. A robust online presence can help you showcase your property's unique offerings and build trust with potential guests.
2. Building a user-friendly website: One of the first steps in establishing a strong online presence is creating a user-friendly and visually appealing website. Ensure your website features high-quality images, detailed property descriptions, and easy-to-navigate booking options, making it simple for guests to learn about your property and make reservations.
3. Leveraging social media platforms: Social media platforms like Facebook, Instagram, and Pinterest can be powerful tools for connecting with potential guests and showcasing your property. Share engaging content, such as behind-the-scenes stories, guest testimonials, and local recommendations, to create a sense of community and showcase your property's unique charm.
4. Reputation management and online reviews: The importance of online reviews cannot be overstated. Actively encourage your guests to leave reviews on platforms like VRBO, Airbnb, and Google, and respond promptly and professionally to both positive and negative feedback. This not only demonstrates your commitment to guest satisfaction but also helps build trust with potential guests browsing online reviews.

By focusing on building a strong online presence and managing your property's reputation, you can attract more guests and enhance their loyalty to your vacation rental. Remember, the key to success in the digital age is staying connected, engaged, and responsive to the ever-evolving needs and preferences of your guests.

As we conclude this chapter, I hope you're feeling inspired and equipped to cultivate lasting guest loyalty and take your vacation rental business to new heights. With these strategies and insights, you're well on your way to creating unforgettable experiences for your guests and securing their loyalty for years to come.

In the upcoming chapters, we'll explore even more strategies and tactics to help you maximize your vacation rental investment and achieve long-term success in this competitive industry. So stay tuned and get ready to embark on an exciting journey of growth and discovery!

FIVE:
Organic Marketing Wonders -
Fresh Approaches to Make Your Property Shine

The Importance of Organic Marketing in the Vacation Rental Industry

1. Going beyond the listing services: It's no secret that many vacation rental owners and managers rely heavily on listing services like VRBO and Airbnb to bring in guests. While these platforms are undoubtedly valuable, it's crucial not to overlook the power of organic marketing in setting your property apart from the competition and attracting a loyal guest base.

2. The pitfalls of being lazy: Simply relying on listing services and local demand can leave your vacation rental vulnerable to fluctuations in the market and the ever-changing algorithms of these platforms. By investing time and effort into organic marketing strategies, you can create a more stable and sustainable source of bookings and revenue for your property.

3. Stand out from the crowd: The vacation rental industry is more competitive than ever, making it essential to differentiate your property from the countless others vying for guest attention. A creative and well-executed organic marketing strategy can help you showcase your property's unique value proposition and make it stand out from the crowd.

Unearthing Hidden Gems in Organic Marketing

1. Tapping into the power of storytelling: One often-overlooked organic marketing strategy is storytelling. Share captivating stories about your property's history, the local community, or the unique experiences your guests can enjoy during their stay. These stories can create an emotional connection with potential guests and pique their interest in booking your property.

2. Collaborating with local businesses and influencers: Another fresh approach to organic marketing involves partnering with local businesses and influencers. By collaborating on events, promotions, or content, you can tap into their audience, build credibility, and generate buzz around your vacation rental property.

3. User-generated content: Encourage your guests to share their experiences at your property on social media, using a specific hashtag or tagging your property's account. This user-generated content can help build social proof, showcase your property from the perspective of actual guests, and expand your reach to potential new guests.

4. SEO and content marketing: While many vacation rental owners may be familiar with the concept of search engine optimization (SEO) and content marketing, there's always room for innovation and improvement. Keep up with the latest trends and best practices in SEO, and create engaging, informative content that addresses the needs and interests of your target audience. This could include blog posts, videos, or even podcasts.

Waking Up to the Potential of Organic Marketing

1. Embracing a proactive mindset: To truly unlock the potential of organic marketing, vacation rental owners and managers must adopt a proactive mindset. Instead of relying on listing services and local demand, take charge of your property's success by actively seeking out and implementing innovative marketing strategies.
2. Continuously learning and evolving: The world of organic marketing is constantly evolving, making it essential for vacation rental professionals to stay informed and adapt their strategies accordingly. By doing so, you can ensure that your property remains at the forefront of industry trends and continues to capture the attention of potential guests.
3. Measuring and optimizing: Lastly, it's crucial to regularly assess the effectiveness of your organic marketing efforts and make adjustments as needed. By tracking key performance indicators (KPIs) and analyzing the data, you can refine your strategies, maximize your return on investment, and ensure the continued growth and success of your vacation rental property.

Hidden Tactics for Extraordinary Organic Marketing

1. Leveraging Google My Business: Many vacation rental owners overlook the power of Google My Business in attracting guests. By creating and optimizing your property's Google My Business listing, you can improve your visibility in local search results, showcase your property through photos and reviews, and make it easier for guests to find and book your property.
2. Harnessing the power of Pinterest: While Pinterest may not be the first platform that comes to mind for vacation rental marketing, its visual nature and focus on travel inspiration make it an ideal place to showcase your property. Create eye-catching, high-quality pins featuring your property, and link them back to your website or booking platform to drive traffic and bookings.
3. Creating immersive virtual experiences: In an age where virtual reality and 360-degree photos are becoming increasingly popular, offering immersive virtual experiences can set your property apart. Invest in creating a virtual tour of your property, and share it on your website and social media channels to give potential guests a taste of what they can expect during their stay.
4. The art of email marketing: Many vacation rental owners underestimate the power of email marketing in building guest loyalty and driving repeat bookings. Collect guests' email addresses (with their permission) and use them to send out personalized, targeted communications, such as special offers, updates on local events, or even a newsletter featuring stories about your property and the surrounding area.
5. Host unique events or experiences: Another way to generate buzz around your vacation rental is by hosting unique events or experiences that cater to your target audience's interests. This could be anything from a wine-tasting or cooking class to a guided hike or photography workshop. By offering

these memorable experiences, you can attract guests who are interested in more than just a place to stay.

6. Cross-promotion with complementary businesses: Seek partnerships with complementary businesses in your area, such as restaurants, tour operators, or attractions. By promoting each other's offerings and providing exclusive discounts or perks to each other's guests, you can tap into a new pool of potential customers and add value to your guests' overall experience.

7. Guest blogging and PR outreach: Establish yourself as an authority in your niche by guest blogging on relevant websites or contributing articles to local publications. This not only builds credibility and trust but also helps drive traffic to your website. Additionally, reach out to journalists and influencers who cover travel or vacation rentals and pitch them unique, newsworthy stories about your property or local area.

As you explore these hidden tactics and continue to evolve your organic marketing strategy, you'll not only set your vacation rental property apart from the competition but also create memorable experiences for your guests that will keep them coming back for more. Remember, the key to success in organic marketing is a combination of creativity, persistence, and a deep understanding of your target audience's needs and desires. Embrace these principles, and watch your vacation rental business soar to new heights.

Tapping into Local Influencers and Professionals for Organic Promotion

1. Real estate agents: Build relationships with local real estate agents who are in contact with potential vacationers and investors. Offer them incentives to recommend your property, such as referral fees or discounts for their clients.
   o Attend local real estate networking events
   o Host open houses or property tours for agents to familiarize them with your vacation rental
   o Create professional, branded materials for agents to share with their clients

2. Tour operators: Partner with local tour operators who can promote your property to their clients as part of their packages or recommend your rental as a convenient and comfortable place to stay.
   o Offer special rates or packages for tour operators' clients
   o Create co-branded marketing materials, such as brochures or flyers
   o Offer incentives for tour operators to refer guests, such as a commission or referral bonus

3. Concierge services: Network with local concierge service providers, as they are often asked for recommendations on where to stay.
   o Offer exclusive discounts or perks for their clients
   o Provide them with promotional materials to share with their clients
   o Collaborate on creating custom experiences for their clients staying at your property

4. Local business owners: Form alliances with local business owners, especially those in the hospitality, food, and entertainment industries, as they can recommend your property to their customers.
   o Offer reciprocal promotions, such as discounts or special offers for each other's customers
   o Share promotional materials in each other's establishments
   o Host joint events or collaborations to cross-promote each other's businesses

5. Wedding planners: Partner with local wedding planners who can recommend your property to couples and their guests looking for accommodations.
   o Offer special rates or packages for wedding guests
   o Create marketing materials targeted at wedding planners and their clients
   o Attend bridal shows and other wedding industry events to network with planners

6. Travel agents: Build relationships with travel agents who specialize in booking vacations to your area. Offer them incentives, such as referral fees or discounts for their clients.
   o Attend travel industry trade shows and conferences
   o Create professional, branded materials for travel agents to share with their clients
   o Offer training or familiarization trips to help travel agents better understand your property and its offerings

7. Event planners: Connect with local event planners who organize conferences, retreats, and other gatherings that may require accommodations for attendees.
   o Offer special group rates or packages for event attendees
   o Collaborate with event planners on promotional materials and marketing efforts
   o Host events at your property to showcase its suitability for group bookings

8. Social media influencers: Identify local social media influencers who can share their experiences at your property with their followers, effectively promoting your vacation rental to a wider audience.
   o Offer complimentary stays or experiences in exchange for social media coverage
   o Collaborate on content creation, such as blog posts, videos, or Instagram stories
   o Leverage their influence by hosting events or gatherings at your property

9. Local journalists and bloggers: Reach out to local journalists and bloggers who cover travel, lifestyle, or local events, and pitch them stories about your property or the surrounding area.
   o Invite them for a complimentary stay or tour of your property
   o Collaborate on content creation or offer exclusive access to newsworthy events or experiences
   o Build long-term relationships for ongoing coverage and promotion

10. Community organizations and clubs: Network with local community organizations and clubs, such as hiking groups, photography clubs, or cultural associations, which may have members looking for accommodations during their events or outings.
    o Offer special rates or packages for club members
    o Sponsor events or activities hosted by the organizations

11. Artists and artisans: Collaborate with local artists and artisans who can showcase their work at your property, attracting attention from their followers and potential guests interested in the local art scene.
    o Host art exhibitions or open studios at your property
    o Commission custom artwork for your rental, promoting the collaboration on social media
    o Offer special packages that include art classes or workshops for guests

12. Sports and fitness professionals: Partner with local sports and fitness professionals, such as surf instructors, yoga teachers, or personal trainers, who can offer unique experiences for your guests.
   o Offer exclusive classes or sessions for guests staying at your property
   o Collaborate on promotional materials that highlight these unique experiences
   o Attend local fitness events and expos to network with potential partners

13. Ecotourism organizations: Join forces with local ecotourism organizations to offer environmentally friendly experiences for your guests, promoting responsible travel and attracting eco-conscious visitors.
   o Offer green amenities or eco-friendly packages for guests
   o Collaborate on promotional materials that highlight your property's commitment to sustainability
   o Attend ecotourism conferences or workshops to stay informed and connected

14. Cooking schools and chefs: Partner with local cooking schools or chefs who can offer unique culinary experiences for your guests, such as cooking classes, wine tastings, or private dining events.
   o Offer exclusive experiences for guests staying at your property
   o Collaborate on promotional materials that highlight these culinary offerings
   o Attend local food festivals or culinary events to network with potential partners

15. Local transportation providers: Build relationships with local transportation providers, such as shuttle services, car rentals, or even bike rental companies, who can recommend your property to their clients.
   o Offer special transportation packages or discounts for guests staying at your property
   o Collaborate on co-branded marketing materials, such as brochures or promotional flyers
   o Attend local transportation industry events to network with potential partners

16. Language schools and teachers: Connect with local language schools or teachers who can offer language classes or immersive experiences for your guests.
   o Offer exclusive language learning experiences for guests staying at your property
   o Collaborate on promotional materials that highlight these educational offerings
   o Attend local language events or expos to network with potential partners

17. Local photographers and videographers: Collaborate with local photographers and videographers who can capture stunning images and videos of your property, as well as local attractions, to share with potential guests.
   o Offer exclusive photo or video packages for guests staying at your property
   o Collaborate on promotional materials that showcase your property and the surrounding area
   o Attend local photography or videography events to network with potential partners

18. Local historians and cultural experts: Partner with local historians and cultural experts who can offer informative and engaging tours or experiences for your guests, adding depth and meaning to their stay.
   o Offer exclusive cultural experiences for guests staying at your property

- o Collaborate on promotional materials that highlight these unique offerings
- o Attend local history or cultural events to network with potential partners

19. Local musicians and performers: Work with local musicians and performers who can entertain your guests or provide a unique cultural experience during their stay.
- o Host live performances or cultural events at your property
- o Offer exclusive packages that include tickets or access to local performances
- o Attend local music or performance events to network with potential partners

20. Volunteer organizations: Partner with local volunteer organizations to offer meaningful, hands-on experiences for your guests who are interested in giving back to the community during their stay.
- o Offer exclusive volunteer opportunities for guests staying at your property
- o Collaborate on promotional materials that highlight these meaningful experiences
- o Attend local volunteer fairs or events to network with potential partners

The Partnership Proposal Letter

In the vacation rental business, partnering with local businesses and influencers can help you stand out from the competition and create unforgettable experiences for your guests. One unique and innovative way to do this is by collaborating with local chefs, restaurant owners, or cooking schools to offer exclusive culinary events for your guests.

The letter provided below is a template for reaching out to potential partners in the culinary industry. This letter should be used as a starting point and tailored to fit the specific circumstances of the partnership you are proposing. Here are some guidelines for using this letter effectively:

1. Research and identify potential partners: Look for local chefs, restaurant owners, or cooking schools that share your commitment to quality and would be a good fit for your vacation rental business. Consider their reputation, specialties, and alignment with your brand.
2. Personalize the letter: Before sending the letter, make sure to customize it with the recipient's name, business, and any other relevant details. Demonstrating that you have taken the time to research their work and understand their unique offerings will help establish a genuine connection.
3. Be clear and concise: Clearly explain the purpose of the partnership and the benefits for both parties. Offer specific examples of how you envision the collaboration working, such as exclusive cooking classes, wine tastings, or private dining events.
4. Be flexible

Subject: Partner with [Your Vacation Rental] for an Exclusive and Unforgettable Culinary Experience

Dear [Chef/Owner's Name],

I hope this message finds you well. My name is [Your Name], and I am the proud owner of [Your Vacation Rental], a luxury vacation rental property in [Location]. Our mission is to provide our guests with unique and unforgettable experiences, ensuring that they create cherished memories during their stay.

We have admired your culinary expertise and the incredible dishes you create at [Chef/Owner's Restaurant or Cooking School]. Your passion for [Local Cuisine] and commitment to using fresh, locally sourced ingredients have truly set you apart in our community. We believe that a collaboration between your [Restaurant/Cooking School] and our vacation rental could provide an unparalleled experience for our mutual clientele.

We would like to propose a partnership in which we offer exclusive cooking classes, wine tastings, or private dining events for our guests, hosted by you or your talented team.

By working together, we can introduce our guests to the rich culinary heritage of [Location] and provide them with an immersive, hands-on experience that they will cherish long after their vacation has ended.

In return, we would be delighted to promote your [Restaurant/Cooking School] through our marketing channels, including our website, social media platforms, and promotional materials.

This partnership would not only benefit both of our businesses but also contribute to the local community by showcasing the incredible culinary talent our region has to offer.

We understand that you may have a busy schedule, but we would be grateful for the opportunity to discuss this collaboration further. If you are interested in exploring this partnership, please feel free to contact me at [Your Phone Number] or [Your Email Address]. I would be more than happy to arrange a meeting at your convenience to discuss our proposal in more detail.

Thank you for considering our partnership proposal. We are excited about the possibility of working together to create truly unforgettable experiences for our guests and promoting the culinary excellence of [Location].

Warm regards,

[Your Name]
[Your Vacation Rental]
[Your Phone Number]
[Your Email Address]

SIX:
Crafting Ambiance with Scents That Entice and Delight

Introduction:
Scent is one of the most powerful and evocative senses we possess. It has the power to transport us to different times and places, trigger memories and emotions, and even affect our behavior. In this chapter, we will explore the science behind scent and how it can be harnessed to create a unique and unforgettable experience for vacation rental guests.

The Secret of Scent:
According to author Luca Turin in The Secret of Scent: Adventures in Perfume and the Science of Smell, scent is a language that speaks directly to our emotions and memories. He argues that the power of scent lies in its ability to bypass the rational part of our brains and communicate directly with the limbic system, which controls our emotions and memories.

The Scent of Desire:
In The Scent of Desire: Discovering Our Enigmatic Sense of Smell, author Rachel Herz explores the complex relationship between scent and desire. She explains that scent is a key factor in sexual attraction and can also influence our mood and behavior in other ways.

Smell: A Very Short Introduction:
In this book, author Matthew Cobb provides a concise and accessible overview of the science of smell. He explains how our sense of smell works, how it evolved, and the ways in which it affects our behavior and perception of the world.

Smellosophy:
Author A. S. Barwich takes a philosophical approach to the study of scent in Smellosophy: What the Nose Tells the Mind. She argues that scent is a deeply meaningful and essential part of our experience of the world, and explores its role in human culture, language, and cognition.

Nose Dive:
Harold McGee's Nose Dive: A Field Guide to the World's Smells is a comprehensive and fascinating exploration of the world of scent. From the chemistry of smell to the cultural significance of different scents, this book is a must-read for anyone interested in the power of scent.

Smells:

In Smells: A Cultural History of Odours in Early Modern Times, author Robert Muchembled explores the cultural significance of scent in early modern Europe. He examines the ways in which different scents were perceived and valued, and how they were used in everyday life and in religious and social rituals.

Scent is a powerful tool that can impact guests' moods and emotions when staying at a vacation rental. But how exactly does scent work?

Scent is detected by olfactory receptors in the nose, which send signals to the brain to interpret the scent. These receptors are incredibly sensitive and can detect even the slightest trace of a scent.

The science behind scent goes beyond just the nose, however. The brain plays a major role in how we perceive and react to scent. When we smell something, the brain associates it with memories, emotions, and even survival instincts.

For example, the smell of fresh-baked cookies may trigger feelings of comfort and nostalgia, while the smell of smoke may trigger a sense of danger and the need to escape.

Understanding the science of scent can help vacation rental owners and managers use it to their advantage. Selecting scents that are associated with positive emotions, positive memories, and can create a more inviting and enjoyable experience for guests.

But how do you choose the right scent?

We'll dive deeper into that in the next section.

Scent is a powerful tool that can impact guests' moods and emotions when staying at a vacation rental. But how exactly does scent work?

Scent is detected by olfactory receptors in the nose, which send signals to the brain to interpret the scent. These receptors are incredibly sensitive and can detect even the slightest trace of a scent.

The science behind scent goes beyond just the nose, however. The brain plays a major role in how we perceive and react to scent. When we smell something, the brain associates it with memories, emotions, and even survival instincts.

For example, the smell of fresh-baked cookies may trigger feelings of comfort and nostalgia, while the smell of smoke may trigger a sense of danger and the need to escape.

Understanding the science of scent can help vacation rental owners and managers use it to their advantage. By selecting scents that are associated with positive emotions and memories, they can create a more inviting and enjoyable experience for guests.

But how do you choose the right scent? We'll dive deeper into that in the next section.

When it comes to selecting scents for a vacation rental, there are a few things to consider. First and foremost, you want to select scents that are pleasant and inviting.

This can vary depending on the location and style of your vacation rental. For example, if your rental is near the ocean, you may want to consider scents that are reminiscent of the beach, such as saltwater or coconut.

You also want to consider the intensity of the scent. Too much scent can be overwhelming and even unpleasant for some guests, while too little scent may not have any effect at all. A good rule of thumb is to aim for a subtle scent that enhances the overall ambiance of the space without overpowering it.

Another factor to consider is the type of scent. There are many different types of scents, including floral, herbal, citrus, and woody. Each type of scent can have a different effect on guests. For example, floral scents can be calming and relaxing, while citrus scents can be invigorating and energizing.

It's also important to consider the time of year and the season when selecting scents. For example, in the winter months, guests may appreciate scents that are warm and comforting, such as cinnamon or vanilla. In the summer months, guests may prefer scents that are refreshing and light, such as lemon or mint.

Ultimately, the goal of using scent in a vacation rental is to create a memorable and enjoyable experience for guests. By taking the time to carefully select scents that enhance the ambiance of the space and create a positive emotional response, owners and managers can set themselves apart and create a loyal following of guests who can't wait to return.

When it comes to creating a fragrance that resonates with your guests, there are several factors to consider. First and foremost, you need to think about the location of your property. Is it situated by the beach or nestled in a forested area? Each environment has its own unique scent profile, and it's important to take this into account when selecting fragrances.

For beachfront properties like those in Maui, we recommend opting for scents that evoke a sense of freshness and cleanliness. Citrus-based fragrances like lemon, lime, and grapefruit work well for this purpose. These scents have a natural ability to cut through odors and refresh the air, making them perfect for use in common areas and bedrooms. Other scents that complement the beachfront ambiance include coconut, vanilla, and ocean breeze.

If your property is situated in a more forested area, on the other hand, scents that evoke a sense of nature and earthiness would be more appropriate. Scents like pine, cedar, and eucalyptus can create a calming and relaxing atmosphere, perfect for guests looking for a break from the hustle and bustle of city life.

Another important factor to consider is the purpose of the scent. Are you looking to create an inviting atmosphere as soon as guests walk in the door, or are you looking to create a calming ambiance for guests to unwind in after a long day exploring the area? For creating a welcoming atmosphere upon arrival, we recommend using a diffuser with a citrus scent. For creating a relaxing atmosphere, lavender is a great choice, as it has been shown to promote relaxation and reduce stress.

Lastly, it's important to choose fragrances that are hypoallergenic and safe for guests to use. This means avoiding fragrances that contain harsh chemicals or synthetic fragrances. Instead, opt for natural and organic scents that are gentle on the senses and safe for guests with allergies or sensitivities.

By taking these factors into consideration, you can create a fragrance experience that resonates with your guests and sets your property apart from the competition.

To enhance the tropical vibe, I recommend using scents like coconut, pineapple, mango, and hibiscus. These scents will transport your guests to a sunny, tropical paradise.

For a more calming effect, lavender, chamomile, and eucalyptus are great choices. Lavender is known for its soothing properties, chamomile is calming and relaxing, and eucalyptus is great for reducing stress and promoting relaxation.

In the bathroom, consider using citrus scents like lemon and grapefruit to create a fresh and clean feeling. These scents are also great for neutralizing odors.

In the bedroom, use scents that promote relaxation and sleep like lavender, vanilla, and sandalwood. These scents will help your guests unwind and get a good night's sleep.

When it comes to the living room, you want to create a warm and inviting atmosphere.
Scents like cinnamon, pumpkin, and apple are perfect for creating a cozy and comfortable environment.

It's also important to consider the intensity of the scent. You don't want to overpower your guests with a strong scent, but at the same time, you want them to notice and appreciate the fragrance. A good rule of thumb is to use a lighter scent in smaller spaces and a stronger scent in larger spaces.

To ensure that your guests have a pleasant experience, it's important to use high-quality, natural scents. Avoid synthetic fragrances as they can be irritating and overwhelming.
In addition to using scents, you can also create a welcoming atmosphere with music, lighting, and décor. But scent is an often-overlooked element that can have a big impact on the overall guest experience. So don't underestimate the power of a good fragrance!

SEVEN:
First Impressions: Designing the Perfect Arrival Experience for Your Guests

In this chapter, we will be discussing how to design the perfect arrival experience for your guests. We know that first impressions are everything and the arrival experience sets the tone for the entire vacation. With our guidance, you will learn how to create a welcoming, relaxing, and unforgettable experience that will have your guests raving about your property for years to come.

We understand that it can be challenging to come up with unique ideas for a first impression that sets your property apart. That's why we've compiled a list of fresh, exciting ideas that will wow your guests and create a lasting impression. Whether it's a simple yet thoughtful gesture or a grandiose display, we have ideas to fit every property and budget.

As you read through this chapter, keep in mind that a first impression doesn't stop at the front door. Every detail from the driveway to the entrance should be carefully considered to make your guests feel welcome and appreciated. With our expertise and your creativity, we can create a first impression that sets your property apart from the rest.

So, sit back, relax, and let's dive into designing the perfect arrival experience for your guests.

As a vacation rental owner, I always want to make sure that my guests have the best possible experience from the moment they arrive at my property. After all, the first impression is often the most lasting.

One way to make sure that guests feel welcome and taken care of is by providing them with a welcome package. This can include anything from a basket of fresh fruit to a bottle of wine, and it's a great way to show your guests that you're thinking of them.

Another way to make a great first impression is by providing your guests with a personalized tour of your property. This not only shows them where everything is located, but it also gives you an opportunity to answer any questions they may have and make sure they feel comfortable in their new surroundings.

It's also important to pay attention to the little details. Making sure that the temperature is comfortable, the lighting is just right, and the décor is welcoming can all contribute to a positive first impression.

One of my favorite ways to create a welcoming atmosphere is by adding fresh flowers or plants to the space. Not only do they add color and fragrance, but they also show that you've put in the extra effort to make your guests feel at home.

Of course, the perfect arrival experience will vary from guest to guest, and it's important to stay flexible and responsive to their needs. But by taking the time to think about their arrival experience and putting in the effort to make it special, you'll set the tone for a memorable and enjoyable stay.

Designing the Perfect Arrival Experience for Your Guests

As a vacation rental owner or manager, you have the opportunity to create a memorable and welcoming arrival experience for your guests. Here are 25 actionable ways to make a great first impression:

1. Provide a welcome package with local maps, brochures, and recommendations for things to do in the area.
2. Use scents to create a welcoming atmosphere, such as a diffuser with a calming essential oil or a candle with a fresh scent.
3. Set the temperature to a comfortable level before guests arrive.
4. Ensure the property is well-lit for evening arrivals.
5. Provide a personalized welcome note or card.
6. Offer a small gift, such as a local treat or a personalized souvenir.
7. Have fresh flowers or plants in the entryway.
8. Make sure the entryway is clean and clutter-free.
9. Consider playing soft background music to create a relaxing atmosphere.
10. Provide a charging station for guests' electronic devices.
11. Offer a complimentary beverage, such as bottled water or a local craft beer.
12. Include a basket of snacks for guests to enjoy upon arrival.
13. Ensure the property is easy to find with clear signage and instructions.
14. Have the key or lockbox easily accessible and well-labeled.
15. Provide a tour of the property upon arrival.
16. Offer a list of amenities available at the property, such as access to a pool or gym.
17. Make sure the property is clean and tidy, with fresh linens and towels.
18. Provide a first aid kit and other emergency supplies.
19. Ensure there are plenty of toiletries, such as soap and shampoo, available for guests.
20. Have a selection of books or board games available for guests to use during their stay.
21. Offer a guide to using the property's appliances and electronics.
22. Provide instructions for using the property's heating and cooling systems.
23. Have a backup plan in case of a power outage or other emergency.
24. Consider offering a concierge service to help guests plan their stay.
25. Follow up with guests after their arrival to ensure everything meets their expectations.

Creating a great first impression for your guests can set the tone for a fantastic vacation experience. By following these tips, you can design the perfect arrival experience and help your guests feel right at home.

To create an unforgettable arrival experience, it's important to understand the psychology behind it. As humans, we're wired to react emotionally to our surroundings, and the way we feel in a new environment can impact our entire experience. Here are some psychological factors to keep in mind when designing your arrival experience:

- The power of first impressions: The first few seconds of an arrival can set the tone for the entire vacation. Creating a welcoming, pleasant, and aesthetically pleasing arrival experience can put your guests in a positive frame of mind right from the start.
- The importance of anticipation: Building anticipation is a key factor in creating a memorable arrival experience. By giving guests a glimpse of what's to come, you can build excitement and anticipation for their stay. This can be done through photos, videos, or even a personalized welcome message.
- The role of sensory experiences: Engaging all the senses can create a truly immersive arrival experience. From the smell of fresh flowers to the sound of calming music, incorporating sensory elements can create a lasting impact and set the tone for a relaxing and enjoyable vacation.
- The impact of personalization: Personalizing the arrival experience can make guests feel special and valued. By catering to their unique preferences and needs, you can create a more memorable and enjoyable experience that will leave a lasting impression.

By understanding these psychological factors, you can create an arrival experience that not only meets your guests' practical needs but also leaves a lasting emotional impact.

EIGHT:
Choosing Your Cleaning Crew: The Insider's Guide to Spotless Success"

When you think of a cleaning company, what comes to mind? Probably just someone who cleans, right? But choosing a cleaning crew for your vacation rental is much more than that. The quality of the cleaning crew you choose can make or break your business.

In this chapter, we'll explore the insider's guide to choosing a cleaning crew that will ensure spotless success for your vacation rental. We'll dive into the importance of choosing the right cleaning crew, the risks of choosing the wrong one, and the impact they can have on your guests' experience.

We'll discuss why your cleaning crew is not just a cleaning crew but an extension of your brand, and how they can help enhance your guests' experience.

So let's get started and learn how to choose the right cleaning crew for your vacation rental.

Part 1: The Importance of Choosing the Right Cleaning Crew

Choosing the right cleaning crew is crucial to the success of your vacation rental business. Here are some reasons why:

1. First Impressions: Your guests' first impression of your property will be based on its cleanliness. A clean property is essential to creating a positive first impression and sets the tone for the rest of the stay.
2. Guest Satisfaction: A clean and well-maintained property will keep your guests happy and satisfied. If they have a bad experience with the cleanliness of your property, it can lead to negative reviews and fewer bookings.
3. Health and Safety: A clean property is essential for the health and safety of your guests. A dirty property can harbor germs and bacteria, which can cause illness and harm.
4. Legal Liability: As a vacation rental owner, you have a legal obligation to provide a safe and clean property for your guests. If your property is not up to standard, it can lead to legal issues and lawsuits.

The Risks of Choosing the Wrong Cleaning Crew

Choosing the wrong cleaning crew for your vacation rental can have serious consequences. Here are some risks you may face:

1. Poor Quality: If you choose a cleaning crew that does not have a high standard of quality, it can lead to negative reviews and lower bookings.
2. Theft and Damage: Hiring an untrustworthy cleaning crew can put your property at risk for theft and damage.
3. Legal Liability: If your cleaning crew is not properly licensed and insured, it can leave you open to legal liability in the event of an accident or injury.

The Impact of Your Cleaning Crew on Guest Experience

Your cleaning crew is not just a cleaning crew; they are an extension of your brand and can have a significant impact on your guests' experience. Here's how:

1. Attention to Detail: A good cleaning crew will pay attention to the small details that can make a big difference in your guests' experience, such as ensuring towels are neatly folded and toilet paper is stocked.
2. Flexibility: A good cleaning crew will be flexible and able to work around your guests' schedules, ensuring a seamless experience for them.
3. Consistency: A good cleaning crew will be consistent in their quality of work, ensuring that your guests' experience is the same every time.
4. Communication: A good cleaning crew will communicate with you regularly to ensure that your property is properly maintained and to address any issues that arise.

How to Choose the Right Cleaning Crew

Choosing the right cleaning crew for your vacation rental is essential. Here are some tips on how to choose the right cleaning crew:

1. Reputation: Look for a cleaning company with a good reputation in the industry and positive reviews from past clients.
2. Experience: Choose a cleaning company with experience in the vacation rental industry, as they will be familiar with the unique needs and requirements of vacation rental properties.
3. Ask for Referrals: Ask for referrals from other vacation rental owners and managers who have had success with a particular cleaning crew. Word of mouth is one of the most reliable ways to find a quality cleaning crew.
4. Look for Professionalism: Look for a cleaning company that is professional, punctual, and reliable. They should have a good reputation in the industry and have the necessary licenses and insurance.
5. Check their Track Record: Look for a cleaning crew with a track record of excellence in their work. You can do this by checking online reviews and testimonials from previous clients.

6. Inquire About Training: Inquire about the level of training and experience of the cleaning crew. A good cleaning crew should be knowledgeable about different types of surfaces, products, and cleaning methods.

7. Understand the Scope of Work: Make sure you understand the scope of work that the cleaning crew will be responsible for. Will they only clean the common areas or will they also clean the bedrooms and bathrooms? Will they handle laundry and linens?

8. Check for Flexibility: Make sure the cleaning crew is flexible and can work around your schedule. They should be able to accommodate last-minute changes or emergency cleaning needs.

9. Communicate Expectations: Communicate your expectations clearly with the cleaning crew. Make sure they understand what you expect from them in terms of the level of cleanliness and the specific tasks they will be responsible for.

10. Provide Feedback: Provide feedback to the cleaning crew on a regular basis. Let them know what they are doing well and where they can improve. This will help them provide better service and improve their overall quality.

11. Discuss Pricing: Discuss pricing with the cleaning crew up front. Make sure you understand their rates and what is included in their service. Compare pricing and services with other cleaning companies to ensure you are getting the best value for your money.

12. Build a Relationship: Build a strong relationship with your cleaning crew. Show appreciation for their hard work and dedication to keeping your vacation rental clean and comfortable for your guests.

13. Consider Green Cleaning: Consider using a cleaning company that uses eco-friendly and non-toxic cleaning products. This not only promotes a healthy environment but also appeals to guests who are environmentally conscious.

14. Address Issues Promptly: Address any issues with the cleaning crew promptly. If there are any areas that need improvement or if there are any complaints from guests, address them immediately with the cleaning crew to ensure they are resolved.

15. Monitor Quality: Regularly monitor the quality of work provided by the cleaning crew. Make sure they are meeting your expectations and delivering the level of cleanliness and service you require.

16. Reward Excellence: Reward the cleaning crew for their excellence in work. Consider bonuses, incentives, or recognition for exceptional service and loyalty.

17. Keep Them Informed: Keep the cleaning crew informed of any changes or updates to the vacation rental property. This includes changes to the layout, furnishings, or amenities that may affect their cleaning procedures.

18. Plan Ahead: Plan ahead for busy seasons and holidays. Make sure you have a cleaning crew in place well in advance to ensure they are available and prepared to handle the increased workload.

19. Monitor Performance Metrics: Use performance metrics to monitor the performance of your cleaning crew. This includes metrics such as guest satisfaction, cleanliness ratings, and turnaround time.

20. Check for References: Check references before hiring a cleaning crew. This includes checking with previous clients to get an idea of their level of satisfaction with the service provided.

21. Emphasize Attention to Detail: Emphasize the importance of attention to detail with your cleaning crew. This includes ensuring that every surface, nook, and cranny is thoroughly cleaned to maintain a high level of cleanliness.

The Right Cleaning Company: Your Right-Hand Man

A great cleaning company is more than just a team of cleaners that make your vacation rental look spotless. They can be your right-hand man in the rental business. A quality cleaning company can not only save you time and hassle, but they can also save you tens of thousands of dollars in the long run.

One of the biggest advantages of having a great cleaning company on your team is that they can often handle tasks that would otherwise require hiring additional service providers. For example, a good cleaning company may be able to fix minor maintenance issues, handle laundry and linens, restock supplies, and even help you stage your property. By bundling these services with their regular cleaning, you save time and money while ensuring that your vacation rental is always ready for guests.

Moreover, the right cleaning company can save you tens of thousands of dollars by helping you avoid costly maintenance issues. A cleaning company that is trained to spot and report issues can help you catch potential problems before they become major headaches. By staying on top of maintenance, you can avoid costly repairs and replacements down the line.

So, when choosing a cleaning company, don't just think of them as a cost. Think of them as an investment in your business. A great cleaning company can be your right-hand man, helping you streamline your rental operations, increase guest satisfaction, and save you money.

Pitfalls of Choosing The Wrong Cleaning Partner

Choosing the right cleaning partner for your vacation rental can make all the difference in the success of your business. It's important to avoid the common pitfalls that can arise when working with the wrong cleaning company. Here are 20 pitfalls to watch out for:

1. Poor communication leading to miscommunication
2. Inconsistent quality of cleaning leading to negative guest reviews
3. Hidden fees that increase costs unexpectedly
4. Lack of availability during peak rental season
5. Lack of reliability leading to last-minute cancellations
6. Unprofessionalism leading to a negative guest experience
7. Inadequate cleaning supplies leading to subpar cleaning results
8. Failure to report damages or issues in a timely manner
9. Lack of experience with short-term rental cleaning
10. Overbooking resulting in unclean rentals for incoming guests
11. Inability to handle large groups or events
12. Lack of proper insurance coverage leading to liability issues
13. Unreliable scheduling and poor time management
14. Failure to follow local regulations and laws
15. Neglecting to clean hard-to-reach areas such as high ceilings or air ducts
16. Poor customer service leading to negative reviews and loss of business
17. Inability to handle emergency cleanings or unexpected issues
18. Subcontracting work to unqualified individuals

19. Lack of attention to detail leading to a lackluster guest experience
20. Ignoring feedback and failing to make necessary improvements

Choosing the right cleaning partner for your vacation rental can be a game-changer. By avoiding these 20 pitfalls, you can ensure that your guests have a positive experience and that your business runs smoothly. Don't settle for subpar cleaning services – invest in a reliable and professional cleaning company that will help you grow your business and avoid unnecessary headaches.

NINE:
The Dynamic Duo: How Staging and Cleaning Go Hand in Hand

As vacation rental owners, we understand the importance of creating a memorable experience for our guests. But to do so, we must first focus on the basics of providing a clean and well-staged rental space. In this chapter, we will delve deep into the concept of staging and cleaning, exploring how they work together to enhance the overall guest experience.

We'll look at the benefits of staging and cleaning, how to implement a successful staging and cleaning program, and the pitfalls to avoid when working with these two essential components. So, let's dive in and discover how the dynamic duo of staging and cleaning can help your vacation rental stand out from the crowd.

Now, let's start with some key points to consider:

1. Staging and cleaning are two essential components of creating an exceptional guest experience.
2. Staging creates an inviting and welcoming atmosphere that sets the tone for the guest's stay.
3. Cleaning provides the foundation for a safe and healthy living environment for guests.
4. The combination of staging and cleaning can increase guest satisfaction and lead to positive reviews and repeat bookings.
5. A well-staged and clean vacation rental can command higher rates and attract a higher caliber of guests.
6. A lack of attention to either staging or cleaning can result in negative guest experiences, negative reviews, and a decrease in bookings.
7. It's important to establish a regular schedule for both staging and cleaning to maintain a consistent level of quality.
8. The use of professional staging and cleaning services can save time, money, and resources in the long run.
9. By investing in the dynamic duo of staging and cleaning, vacation rental owners can ensure a successful and profitable business.

Now, let's expand on each of these points and dive deeper into the importance of staging and cleaning in the vacation rental industry.

To make the most out of staging and cleaning, it is important to establish a consistent and efficient workflow. This involves setting up a checklist of tasks that need to be completed before and after each guest's stay.

Before the guest's arrival, the cleaning crew should perform a thorough cleaning of the property, paying close attention to high-traffic areas, appliances, and surfaces. This includes vacuuming, dusting, cleaning the bathrooms, and wiping down all surfaces. It is important to use high-quality cleaning products and equipment to ensure a deep clean and maintain the property's condition.

Once the cleaning is complete, it's time to stage the property. This involves arranging the furniture, adding decorative elements, and making sure that everything is in place and ready for the guest's arrival. The goal is to create an inviting and comfortable space that feels like a home away from home.

To achieve this, it's important to consider the needs and preferences of the target market. For example, if the property is geared towards families with young children, it may be helpful to provide baby equipment, such as a high chair or crib. Alternatively, if the property is aimed at couples or business travelers, it may be beneficial to provide amenities such as a work desk or a cozy reading nook.

During the guest's stay, it's important to maintain the property's cleanliness and appearance. This involves performing regular cleanings and touch-ups, as well as addressing any issues or concerns that may arise. It's also important to provide a seamless and hassle-free experience for the guest, from check-in to check-out.

After the guest's departure, the cleaning crew should perform a thorough cleaning of the property once again, ensuring that everything is in top condition for the next guest's arrival. This includes washing and changing linens, disinfecting surfaces, and performing any necessary repairs or maintenance.

To ensure that the staging and cleaning process is as effective and efficient as possible, it's important to establish clear communication and expectations with the cleaning crew and staging team. This involves providing detailed instructions and checklists, as well as regular feedback and performance evaluations.

In conclusion, the dynamic duo of staging and cleaning is essential to creating a successful vacation rental business. By establishing a consistent and efficient workflow, and paying close attention to the needs and preferences of the target market, owners and managers can create an inviting and comfortable space that guests will love. With a strong focus on quality and attention to detail, a well-staged and maintained vacation rental can lead to repeat business, positive reviews, and a loyal customer base.

When it comes to vacation rental management, there are two essential elements that work in harmony to create the perfect guest experience: staging and cleaning. Both are crucial components that should be carefully considered and executed to achieve optimal results.

In this section, we'll delve deeper into the relationship between these two elements, exploring the ways in which they work together to enhance the overall guest experience. We'll provide insights into the benefits of proper staging and cleaning, as well as tips and techniques for maximizing the impact of both.

By the end of this chapter, you'll have a solid understanding of how the dynamic duo of staging and cleaning can elevate your vacation rental to the next level.

- Understand the Power of Perception: Perception is everything when it comes to vacation rentals. Guests make snap judgments about the cleanliness and appeal of a property within seconds of entering. By staging and cleaning your vacation rental, you're creating a positive perception that can influence a guest's entire stay.

- Use Staging to Enhance Your Property's Features: Staging is about more than just making a space look pretty. It's about strategically placing furniture, artwork, and other decors to enhance the natural beauty and features of your property. For example, you can use a large mirror to reflect a beautiful view or place a cozy rug in front of a fireplace to create a welcoming atmosphere.

- Pay Attention to Lighting: Lighting can have a significant impact on how a space feels. A well-lit room feels open and inviting, while a dimly lit space can feel cramped and uninviting. Use a combination of natural and artificial light to create a warm and inviting atmosphere.

- Keep It Simple: When it comes to staging and cleaning, less is often more. Don't clutter your vacation rental with too many decorative items or personal belongings. Instead, create a minimalist look that allows guests to envision themselves in the space.

- Highlight Unique Features: Does your vacation rental have a stunning view, a beautiful fireplace, or a unique architectural feature? Highlight these elements with strategic staging and cleaning techniques to make your property stand out from the competition.

- Make the Most of Outdoor Spaces: If your vacation rental has a balcony, patio, or outdoor living space, make sure it's clean and inviting. Use outdoor furniture, lighting, and decor to create an outdoor oasis that guests will love.

- Use Scent to Enhance the Guest Experience: We've already talked about the power of scent, but it's worth repeating. A pleasant scent can create a welcoming atmosphere and enhance the guest experience. Use candles, diffusers, or other scent products to create a warm and inviting aroma.

- Stay Current with Design Trends: Design trends are constantly evolving, and it's important to stay current with the latest styles and trends. This doesn't mean you need to completely overhaul your vacation rental every season, but it does mean staying aware of current design trends and making small updates as needed.

- Consider Professional Staging Services: If you're not confident in your staging abilities, consider hiring a professional staging company. A professional stager can help you create a cohesive and inviting look that will appeal to a wide range of guests.

- Invest in Quality Cleaning Products: When it comes to cleaning, quality matters. Invest in high-quality cleaning products and equipment to ensure that your vacation rental is spotless and inviting.

- Develop a Cleaning Schedule: A cleaning schedule is essential for keeping your vacation rental in top shape. Create a schedule that outlines daily, weekly, and monthly cleaning tasks, and stick to it.

- Don't Forget the Details: Details matter when it comes to staging and cleaning. Pay attention to small details like dusting light fixtures, cleaning baseboards, and removing cobwebs.

- Get Feedback from Guests: Finally, don't be afraid to ask for feedback from your guests. Ask them what they liked about the property, and what could be improved. This feedback can help you make changes and improvements to your staging and cleaning efforts, ensuring that your vacation rental is always at its best.

Remember, staging and cleaning are essential components of a successful vacation rental business. By following these tips and insights, you can create a welcoming and inviting space that guests will love.

As much as staging and cleaning are crucial components of creating a memorable and satisfying vacation rental experience, their significance transcends the practical or functional domain of housekeeping.

They are also deeply embedded in the psychological and emotional realm of human perception, behavior, and interaction. A vacation rental that is not only clean but also aesthetically pleasing, inviting, and comfortable can trigger positive emotional responses, enhance guest satisfaction, and influence their future behavior, such as repeat bookings or referrals.

The Science Behind Staging: How Our Minds Interpret Space
Numerous studies have examined the effects of environmental stimuli on human behavior and cognition, including the impact of cleanliness, orderliness, and aesthetic appeal on various dimensions of well-being and performance.

For instance, research has shown that exposure to clean and pleasant environments can reduce stress, anxiety, and aggression and improve mood, cognitive functioning, and prosocial behavior (Korpela, 2018; Tennessen & Cimprich, 1995).

Conversely, exposure to messy, cluttered, or disorganized environments can impair cognitive processing, increase stress, and elicit negative affect (Boyce et al., 2010; Lohr et al., 1996).

In the context of vacation rentals, these findings suggest that investing in high-quality cleaning and staging can not only create a favorable impression on guests but also contribute to their physical and psychological well-being during their stay.

By removing physical and sensory barriers that impede relaxation, enjoyment, and socialization, a well-maintained and thoughtfully designed vacation rental can promote a sense of comfort, safety, and harmony that translates into positive attitudes and behaviors.

Moreover, the psychological effects of staging and cleaning go beyond the immediate experience of guests and extend to their memories, perceptions, and intentions. Research has shown that the aesthetic and sensory features of a space can influence how people remember and evaluate it, as well as how likely they are to engage in certain behaviors related to it (Cromley & Azevedo, 2007; Russell & Ward, 1982).

For example, a clean and stylishly decorated vacation rental may enhance guests' recall of positive experiences, increase their perceived value of the rental, and motivate them to recommend it to others or return to it in the future.

Furthermore, staging and cleaning can also act as powerful signaling mechanisms that convey information about the owner or manager's level of care, professionalism, and attention to detail. In the context of the sharing economy and the increasing competition among vacation rentals, these signals can make a significant difference in how guests perceive and choose their preferred accommodation.

By investing in quality cleaning and staging, owners and managers can communicate to their guests that they value their comfort, health, and satisfaction and that they are committed to providing a superior service that exceeds their expectations.

In sum, the psychology behind staging and cleaning in vacation rentals is multifaceted and complex, encompassing a wide range of cognitive, emotional, and social factors that shape guest experiences and behaviors.

By understanding and leveraging these factors, owners, and managers can not only enhance the physical and functional aspects of their rental but also create a memorable, enjoyable, and satisfying experience that resonates with their guests long after their stay.

As I reflect on the dynamic duo of staging and cleaning, I can't help but feel excited about the possibilities. The power of a well-designed, clean, and welcoming space is truly transformative. It can elevate an ordinary experience into an extraordinary one, and create memories that last a lifetime.

But beyond that, there's something deeper at play here. The psychology of space and how it impacts our well-being is a topic that has fascinated me for years.

It's why I'm so passionate about what I do, and why I'm committed to helping others create spaces that inspire, uplift, and nurture.

As vacation rental owners and managers, we have the incredible opportunity to shape the experiences of our guests. We can create spaces that are not just beautiful, but functional, comfortable, and inviting. We can create environments that foster connection, relaxation, and rejuvenation.

But in order to do that, we need to understand the power of staging and cleaning. We need to approach it not as a chore, but as an opportunity to create something truly special. We need to be intentional, thoughtful, and strategic in our approach.

So let me leave you with this: don't underestimate the power of a well-staged, impeccably clean space. It can transform your vacation rental from a forgettable experience into one that your guests will cherish forever. And in doing so, can transform your business and your life.

TEN:
Rave Reviews: Innovative Strategies to Garner Glowing Testimonials

Online reviews are one of the most powerful tools in the vacation rental industry. Positive reviews can lead to increased bookings and revenue, while negative reviews can have the opposite effect. In this chapter, we will explore innovative strategies to help you generate glowing testimonials for your vacation rental property.

1. Encourage Feedback: Encourage guests to provide feedback on their experience. This can be done through an email survey, a comment card, or a follow-up call after their stay. By actively seeking feedback, you show that you value your guests 'opinions and are committed to providing the best possible experience.
2. Make it Easy: Make it easy for guests to leave a review. Include links to your property's review pages in your follow-up emails, on your website, and in your social media posts.
3. Respond to Reviews: Respond to reviews in a timely and professional manner. This shows that you are engaged with your guests and are committed to addressing any concerns they may have.
4. Highlight Positive Reviews: Highlight positive reviews on your website, social media, and marketing materials. This can help to build trust and credibility with potential guests.
5. Use Visuals: Use visuals to showcase your property and its amenities. This can include photos, videos, and virtual tours. Visuals can help to give guests a better sense of what to expect and can help to set realistic expectations.
6. Offer Incentives: Offer incentives for guests who leave reviews. This can include discounts on future stays, gift cards, or other rewards.
7. Use Social Media: Use social media to engage with your guests and encourage them to leave reviews. Share photos and stories from your guests and respond to their comments and questions.
8. Ask for Specific Feedback: Ask guests for specific feedback on different aspects of their stay. This can help you to identify areas for improvement and can help to show that you are committed to providing the best possible experience.
9. Provide Excellent Service: Provide excellent service to your guests from the moment they book until the moment they leave. By providing an exceptional experience, you increase the likelihood that they will leave a positive review.
10. Monitor Your Reviews: Monitor your reviews on a regular basis. This can help you to identify trends and patterns in your guests 'feedback and can help you to address any issues that may arise.

11. Follow Up: Follow up with guests after their stay to thank them for their feedback and to address any concerns they may have raised. This shows that you value their opinions and are committed to making improvements where necessary.

12. Be Authentic: Be authentic in your responses to reviews. Avoid using canned responses and show genuine concern and appreciation for your guests 'feedback.

13. Engage with Influencers: Engage with influencers in your industry and ask them to share their experiences of your property with their followers. This can help to increase your visibility and credibility in the industry.

14. Showcase Unique Features: Showcase unique features of your property that set it apart from others in the area. This can help to generate interest and encourage guests to leave positive reviews.

15. Leverage Repeat Guests: Leverage repeat guests by asking them to leave reviews after their stay. Repeat guests are often more loyal and invested in your property and are more likely to leave positive reviews.

16. Provide a Personal Touch: Provide a personal touch to your guests 'experience. This can include welcome notes, personalized recommendations, and other small gestures that show you care.

17. Use Influencer Marketing: Use influencer marketing to reach a wider audience and encourage them to leave reviews. This can include partnering with influencers in your industry or offering incentives for guests who share their experiences on social media.

18. Follow Up: Follow up with your guests after their stay to see if they enjoyed their experience and encourage them to leave a review. You can send a personalized email or message thanking them for choosing your vacation rental and kindly asking them to share their experience with others.

19. Make it Easy: Make it as easy as possible for guests to leave a review. Provide them with direct links to your review pages on various platforms, and consider adding a review widget to your website.

20. Offer Incentives: Consider offering incentives for guests who leave a review. This can include a discount on a future stay, a complimentary service or amenity, or a chance to win a prize.

21. Respond to Reviews: Respond to both positive and negative reviews in a timely and professional manner. This shows that you value your guests' feedback and are committed to providing excellent service.

22. Learn from Feedback: Use guest feedback to improve your vacation rental and the guest experience. Identify areas for improvement and take action to address any issues raised in reviews.

23. Promote Your Reviews: Promote your positive reviews on social media and your website. This can help attract new guests and build trust with potential customers.

24. Monitor Your Reputation: Regularly monitor your online reputation to see what guests are saying about your vacation rental. This includes checking review sites and social media platforms for feedback.

25. Don't Fake It: Don't fake reviews or encourage guests to write false reviews. This is unethical and can damage your reputation in the long run.

Overall, generating rave reviews is all about providing a great guest experience, communicating effectively with your guests, and leveraging the power of online platforms to promote your vacation rental. By following these strategies, you can generate glowing testimonials and build a strong reputation in the vacation rental industry.

Catch Them in the Moment:

The key to getting glowing testimonials is catching your guests in the moment. After they've enjoyed a great experience, it's important to ask them how their stay was and if there was anything they would have liked to have seen differently. This gives you the opportunity to address any issues that might have come up and make things right before they have a chance to leave a negative review.

Create a Two-Step Process: Instead of immediately asking guests to leave a review, create a two-step process that first involves a quick and informal follow-up conversation. This can be done via email or phone, and can include questions like "How was your stay with us?" or "Was there anything we could have done to improve your experience?"

Direct Happy Guests to Review Sites: If the guest responds positively, you can then direct them to leave a review on your preferred review site. Make it easy for them by providing links or QR codes, and consider offering a small incentive for leaving a review. This can be something as simple as a discount on their next stay or a small gift card to a local restaurant.

Address Negative Feedback: If the guest has any negative feedback, it's important to address it immediately and do everything you can to make things right. This shows the guest that you care about their experience and are committed to providing a great stay. Once the issue has been resolved, you can then ask if they would be willing to leave a review.

Monitor Your Online Presence: Keep an eye on your online reviews and respond to both positive and negative feedback. Thank guests for their positive comments and address any negative feedback with a genuine apology and a plan for how you will improve in the future.

Encourage Repeat Business: Remember that happy guests are more likely to leave positive reviews and to return for future stays. Make sure to follow up with them after their stay, offer incentives for repeat business, and provide exceptional service every time they visit.

By following these simple steps and creating a two-step process for generating reviews, you can ensure that your guests have a great experience and that your online presence is filled with positive feedback.

How to Get Valuable Feedback from Your Guests" or "The Art of Asking for Feedback: A Proven Template

As a vacation rental owner or manager, it's essential to keep open communication with your guests even after their stay. One way to do this is by sending a follow-up letter requesting feedback on their experience.

Not only does this show that you value their opinion, but it can also provide valuable insights for future improvements. In this section, we have provided a sample letter template that you can use to ask for a response from your guests.

The goal of this letter is to gather information on their experience so that you can address any issues and make improvements to your vacation rental.

Subject: Let us know how your stay was…
Dear [guest name],

We hope you had a wonderful time during your recent stay with us at [property name]. We wanted to follow up with you and see how everything went. Your feedback is important to us, as it helps us continue to provide excellent service to our guests.

If you have a few minutes, we would appreciate it if you could let us know about your experience. We would like to know what you liked and what we can improve on for future guests.

Please feel free to respond to this email with your thoughts or comments. We would love to hear from you.

Thank you for choosing to stay with us, and we hope to see you again soon!

Best regards,

[Your name]

We understand that not every guest has a positive experience, and that's okay. In our next chapter, we'll discuss what to do if you receive negative feedback and how to handle it professionally.

But for now, we hope to hear from you soon about your recent stay with us. Your feedback is invaluable in helping us improve our services and create an even better experience for our guests.

What to Do When Guests Complain: A Comprehensive Guide for Property Owners
As a property owner or manager, receiving complaints from guests is inevitable. While most guests are satisfied with their stay, there may be times when something goes wrong or a guest is unhappy with their experience.

How you respond to guest complaints can make a huge difference in the guest's satisfaction, the reputation of your property, and the success of your business. In this guide, we'll provide you with 20 actionable steps you can take to address guest complaints effectively and ensure guest satisfaction.

20 Steps to Address Guest Complaints:

1. Listen attentively to the guest's complaint
2. Apologize sincerely for the inconvenience caused
3. Take ownership of the problem and assure the guest that you will resolve it
4. Ask questions to understand the root cause of the problem
5. Offer a solution or compensation that meets the guest's needs

6. Follow up with the guest to ensure the issue has been resolved to their satisfaction
7. Document the complaint and the steps taken to resolve it
8. Train your staff to handle complaints effectively and provide them with the tools and resources they need
9. Implement a guest feedback system to proactively identify and address issues before they become complaints
10. Respond to complaints promptly, ideally within 24 hours
11. Empower your staff to make decisions and take action to resolve complaints
12. Use positive language and tone when communicating with guests
13. Take steps to prevent the issue from happening again in the future
14. Offer a genuine and heartfelt apology when necessary
15. Be transparent and honest with guests about the issue and what steps you are taking to resolve it
16. Provide compensation that is appropriate and fair for the situation
17. Show empathy and understanding toward the guest's situation
18. Use the complaint as an opportunity to improve your business
19. Follow up with the guest after their stay to ensure their overall satisfaction
20. Continuously review and improve your complaint-handling process

By implementing these 20 steps, you can effectively address guest complaints and ensure guest satisfaction.

Remember, guest complaints are an opportunity for you to improve your business and build strong relationships with your guests.

By taking the time to listen, understand, and address their concerns, you can turn a negative experience into a positive one and create loyal customers for life.

As important as it is to address negative feedback, it's equally important to leverage positive feedback and turn it into third-party reviews. These reviews are essential for building your business's reputation and attracting new guests. So, let's dive into how to handle positive replies and encourage your guests to leave reviews.

Turning Positive Feedback into Powerful 3rd Party Reviews: A Step-by-Step Guide

Positive feedback is always great to receive, but it's important to take that positive energy and use it to your advantage. In this guide, we'll cover how to handle positive replies and turn them into powerful third-party reviews.

By following these simple steps, you'll be able to showcase your guests' satisfaction and attract new guests to your property.

Example Letter Template:

Dear [Guest Name],

Thank you for choosing [Property Name] as your destination. We're thrilled to hear that you had a great experience with us and we appreciate you taking the time to share your feedback.

Your positive feedback means a lot to us, and we'd like to invite you to share your experience on [Review Site]. Your review will help us showcase our commitment to providing exceptional service to our guests, and it will help other travelers choose our property for their next stay.

To leave a review, simply visit [Review Site] and share your experience. Your review will be visible to other travelers, and it will help us improve our services.

Once again, thank you for choosing [Property Name] and we look forward to welcoming you back in the future.

Best regards,

[Your Name]

Turning positive feedback into third-party reviews is an essential part of building your business's reputation.

By following these simple steps and using our example letter template, you can encourage your guests to share their positive experiences and attract new guests to your property.

Remember, positive reviews are powerful tools for building your business, so don't hesitate to ask your guests to share their satisfaction with the world.

The Ultimate Guide to Review Sites for Vacation Rentals

As a vacation rental owner or manager, you know how important reviews are for your business. Positive reviews can lead to more bookings and a better reputation, while negative reviews can have the opposite effect.

With so many review sites out there, it can be hard to know which ones are worth your time and effort. In this guide, we'll go over the most popular review sites for vacation rentals and provide a brief overview of their pros and cons.

Airbnb

Airbnb is one of the most popular vacation rental review sites, with millions of users worldwide. As an owner or manager, you can respond to reviews and even dispute them if necessary. The site also offers a messaging system that allows you to communicate directly with guests.

Pros: Large user base, ability to respond to reviews, messaging system.

Cons: Review system can be skewed towards positive reviews, dispute process can be time-consuming.

TripAdvisor

TripAdvisor is a well-known travel review site that includes vacation rentals as one of its categories. The site features a review system, as well as a Q&A section where guests can ask questions about the property.

Pros: Large user base, Q&A section, ability to respond to reviews.

Cons: Review systems can be skewed towards negative reviews, and may not be as popular for vacation rentals as other sites.

VRBO/HomeAway

VRBO/HomeAway is a popular vacation rental listing site that also includes a review system. As an owner or manager, you can respond to reviews and even offer discounts to guests who leave a review.

Pros: Large user base, ability to respond to reviews, incentive program.

Cons: Review systems can be skewed towards negative reviews, and may not be as popular for certain destinations.

Google Reviews

Google Reviews is a general review site that can be useful for vacation rentals. Many guests may search for vacation rentals on Google and leave a review there. As an owner or manager, you can respond to reviews and even dispute them if necessary.

Pros: Large user base, ability to respond to reviews, high visibility on Google search results.

Cons: Review systems can be skewed towards negative reviews, and may not be as popular for vacation rentals specifically.

Yelp

Yelp is a popular review site for restaurants and other local businesses, but it can also be useful for vacation rentals. Guests may leave a review of the rental property, and as an owner or manager, you can respond to reviews and even offer discounts to guests who leave a review.

Pros: Large user base, ability to respond to reviews, incentive program.

Cons: Review systems can be skewed towards negative reviews, and may not be as popular for vacation rentals specifically.

In conclusion, reviews are a vital part of the vacation rental industry. They provide valuable feedback to owners and managers, help guests make informed decisions, and can significantly impact a property's visibility and booking rate.

While it's easy to get caught up in the number of positive reviews you receive, it's important to remember that there's always room for improvement. Even the most successful vacation rentals can benefit from new reviews and feedback, as they help to build trust and credibility with potential guests.

Consider these statistics: 97% of travelers read reviews before booking a vacation rental, and 93% say that reviews have a significant impact on their booking decisions. What's more, properties with at least 40 reviews receive 67% more bookings than those with fewer than 10 reviews.

With such a high demand for reviews, it's important to take proactive steps to encourage guests to share their experiences on third-party review sites.

By utilizing the tips and strategies outlined in this article, you can start generating more reviews and building a strong online reputation for your vacation rental business. Remember, it's never too late to start improving your review profile, so don't be afraid to ask for feedback and take action on the suggestions you receive.

With the right approach, you can turn even the toughest critics into loyal advocates for your property.

ELEVEN:
Unlocking the Secrets of VRBO and Airbnb:Tips to Outshine Your Competition

If you're in the vacation rental business, you know that competition is fierce. With the rise of popular online marketplaces like Airbnb and VRBO, it's become more challenging than ever to stand out and attract guests to your property.

In this chapter, we'll share some insider tips and tricks to help you unlock the secrets of Airbnb and VRBO and outshine your competition.

From optimizing your listing to pricing strategies and communication tips, we'll cover everything you need to know to succeed in this competitive industry. So, let's get started and take your vacation rental business to the next level!

Welcome to the world of vacation rentals on VRBO and Airbnb, where competition can be fierce. With so many properties available, it can be challenging to stand out from the crowd and get the bookings you need to make your rental business successful.

But fear not, with the right tips and tricks, you can take your vacation rental property to the next level and outshine your competition.

In this chapter, we'll share some of the secrets to success on VRBO and Airbnb, so you can maximize your visibility, increase your bookings, and achieve your business goals.

Tip #1: Optimize Your Listing
The first step to outshining your competition on VRBO and Airbnb is to optimize your listing. This means making sure your property description is clear and concise, highlighting your unique selling points, and including plenty of high-quality photos that showcase your property in the best possible light.

Consider investing in professional photography to capture the true essence of your property, and make sure to highlight any unique features, such as a stunning view or a luxurious pool. You should also include detailed information about the location, nearby attractions, and amenities, so potential guests can get a clear sense of what they can expect from their stay.

Tip #2: Price Competitively
Price is a key factor when it comes to vacation rental bookings, and it's essential to ensure your property is priced competitively. Research similar properties in your area and see how they are priced, then adjust your rates accordingly.

But keep in mind, it's not always about being the cheapest option. Many guests are willing to pay more for a property that offers exceptional value, so make sure to highlight the benefits of your property and what sets it apart from the rest.

Tip #3: Respond Quickly and Professionally
Guests on VRBO and Airbnb expect quick and professional responses to their inquiries and bookings, so it's essential to respond promptly and with a friendly and professional tone. Make sure to answer any questions they may have and provide all the information they need to make an informed decision about booking your property.

Tip #4: Provide Exceptional Guest Experiences
One of the most effective ways to outshine your competition on VRBO and Airbnb is to provide exceptional guest experiences. This means going above and beyond to ensure your guests have a memorable stay and want to come back again in the future.

Consider providing thoughtful amenities such as welcome baskets, providing a guidebook with local recommendations, or offering a personalized welcome message. By providing exceptional experiences, you'll not only encourage repeat bookings but also increase your chances of positive reviews and word-of-mouth recommendations.

Tip #5: Stay Up-to-Date with Industry Trends
The vacation rental industry is constantly evolving, so it's essential to stay up-to-date with the latest trends and best practices. Subscribe to industry newsletters, join relevant forums or groups, and attend conferences or events to network with other rental owners and gain valuable insights into the industry.

By staying informed and ahead of the curve, you'll be able to make informed decisions about your rental business and adapt to changing trends and guest preferences.

In addition to optimizing your listing and pricing strategy, there are several other tips and tricks you can use to outshine your competition on vacation rental platforms like VRBO and Airbnb.

From creating a unique and memorable guest experience to leveraging the power of social media, these strategies can help you attract more guests, boost your ratings and reviews, and ultimately increase your revenue.

Perfect your property description: Your property description is the first thing potential guests will read, so make sure it's eye-catching and informative. Highlight the unique features of your property, such as stunning views or luxurious amenities, and be sure to include information about the surrounding area and local attractions.

1. Take high-quality photos: Your photos should showcase your property in the best possible light. Use a high-quality camera or hire a professional photographer to capture your space at its best. Make sure to take photos of all the important features, including bedrooms, bathrooms, living areas, and outdoor spaces.
2. Optimize your pricing strategy: Pricing your rental correctly can have a huge impact on your bookings. Take into account the time of year, local events, and demand for your area when setting your rates. Consider offering discounts for longer stays or last-minute bookings to fill gaps in your calendar.
3. Build your reputation: Good reviews are essential for attracting new guests and building your reputation on VRBO and Airbnb. Encourage guests to leave reviews by providing a memorable experience and excellent customer service. Respond promptly and professionally to any negative reviews, and use them as an opportunity to improve your rental.
4. Offer unique experiences: To stand out from the competition, consider offering unique experiences to your guests. This could include local tours or activities, special amenities or services, or a customized welcome package.
5. Use social media to your advantage: Social media is a powerful tool for promoting your rental and connecting with potential guests. Use platforms like Facebook and Instagram to showcase your property and highlight local attractions and events.
6. Stay up-to-date on industry trends: The vacation rental industry is constantly evolving, so it's important to stay informed about new trends and changes. Attend industry events and conferences, network with other owners, and follow industry blogs and news sources to stay on top of the latest developments.

With these tips and strategies, you'll be well on your way to outshining the competition on VRBO and Airbnb.

The Hidden Gems of Vacation Rental Competition: Unseen Opportunities to Outshine Your Rivals

In a competitive vacation rental market, it can be challenging to stand out from the crowd. While you may be doing many things right, there may be some hidden opportunities that your competitors are missing.

In this chapter, we'll explore some of the lesser-known tactics and strategies that can help you outshine your rivals and attract more guests to your vacation rental.

1. Offer a welcome package: Surprise your guests with a welcome package that includes local treats, maps, and guides. This personal touch can make a big difference in their overall experience.
2. Personalize your communication: Use guest data to personalize communication and offer relevant recommendations, such as local restaurants and activities.

3. Provide a local phone number: Offering a local phone number can help guests feel more connected to the area and give them a sense of security.
4. Add a unique amenity: Consider adding a unique amenity that your competitors don't have, such as a hot tub, a game room, or a private beach.
5. Host a local event: Hosting a local event, such as a wine tasting or a cooking class, can attract guests and build goodwill in the community.
6. Focus on sustainability: Incorporating sustainable practices, such as using green cleaning products and installing energy-efficient appliances, can appeal to environmentally-conscious guests.
7. Create a themed rental: Create a themed rental that reflects the local culture or history. This can be a fun and unique experience for guests.
8. Offer add-ons: Consider offering add-ons, such as a grocery delivery service or a private chef, to enhance your guests' stay.
9. Update your listing regularly: Keep your listing up-to-date with fresh photos, updated descriptions, and accurate pricing information.
10. Provide detailed check-in instructions: Provide detailed check-in instructions, including photos and maps, to make the check-in process as smooth as possible.
11. Use video marketing: Use video to showcase your rental and its unique features. This can be a powerful tool for attracting guests and setting yourself apart from the competition.
12. Host a live tour: Consider hosting a live tour of your rental on social media to give potential guests a sneak peek and generate buzz.
13. Respond quickly to inquiries: Respond quickly to inquiries and provide helpful information to show your guests that you value their business.
14. Use dynamic pricing: Use dynamic pricing to adjust your rates based on demand, seasonality, and other factors. This can help you stay competitive and attract more bookings.
15. Offer loyalty rewards: Consider offering loyalty rewards, such as discounts or upgrades, to repeat guests. This can help build loyalty and encourage repeat business.

By focusing on these hidden gems of vacation rental competition, you can differentiate yourself from your rivals and attract more guests to your rental.

Remember, it's the little things that can make a big difference, so be creative and keep exploring new opportunities to stand out in the market.

The Psychology of Complacency: How Vacation Rental Owners and Managers Fall into a Comfortable Rut

As a vacation rental owner or manager, it can be easy to fall into a comfortable routine once your property is established and running smoothly. However, this complacency can lead to missed opportunities and stagnation in a competitive industry.
Understanding the psychology behind complacency can help you recognize the warning signs and prevent it from hindering your success.

Things worth knowing

1. The Comfort Zone Trap: Studies have shown that people have a natural inclination to stay in their comfort zone, which can prevent them from taking risks and trying new things. This can be especially true for vacation rental owners and managers who have found a system that works for them.

2. Fear of Failure: Another psychological factor that can contribute to complacency is a fear of failure. Owners and managers may be hesitant to try new strategies or take risks for fear of negative consequences.

3. Confirmation Bias: This is the tendency to seek out information that confirms our existing beliefs and overlook information that contradicts them. In the vacation rental industry, this can lead to sticking with old methods that have worked in the past instead of exploring new opportunities.

4. Loss Aversion: This is the tendency to place more weight on avoiding losses than on achieving gains. Owners and managers may be more concerned with avoiding negative reviews or losing bookings than with taking steps to improve and grow their business.

5. Learned Helplessness: This is the belief that one's actions have no impact on the outcome of a situation. Owners and managers who feel helpless to improve their business may become complacent and resigned to their current situation.

While complacency can be a natural response to success, it is important for vacation rental owners and managers to recognize the warning signs and avoid falling into a comfortable rut.

By understanding the psychology behind complacency, you can identify areas for improvement and capitalize on opportunities that your competitors may be overlooking. Remember, their downfall can be your opportunity for growth and success in the vacation rental industry.

Congratulations! You've now unlocked the secrets to outshine your competition on VRBO and Airbnb.

By following the tips and techniques outlined in this chapter, you have gained the tools you need to stand out in a crowded vacation rental market.

But remember, success is not a one-time achievement. It's a continuous journey that requires you to stay on top of the latest trends, adapt to changing circumstances, and always be looking for ways to improve.

Keep in mind that complacency and laziness are the enemies of success.

It's easy to fall into the trap of thinking you have it all figured out and becoming comfortable with the status quo. But that's a recipe for stagnation and decline.

Instead, use your newfound knowledge and competitive edge to constantly innovate and improve your vacation rental business.

Keep a finger on the pulse of the market and listen to your guests' feedback to stay ahead of the curve.

And always remember, your competitors' downfall is your opportunity. By staying focused, driven, and constantly improving, you can continue to outshine the competition and achieve the success you deserve.
So go out there and make it happen! The world of vacation rentals is waiting for you.

TWELVE:
The Power of Referrals: Creative Ways to Get Guests Talking About Your Property.

Word-of-mouth marketing is one of the most powerful ways to grow your vacation rental business.

Happy guests who share their positive experiences with others can generate a steady stream of referrals for your property. In this chapter, we'll explore creative ways to get your guests talking about your property and referring others to stay with you.

From referral programs to personalized touches and social media strategies, we'll show you how to leverage the power of referrals to drive more bookings and increase your revenue. So, let's get started!

Revolutionizing Referrals: Innovative Techniques to Supercharge Your Guest Referral Game"

Word of mouth is one of the most powerful forms of advertising out there. People trust recommendations from friends and family far more than they trust traditional advertising. In the vacation rental industry, referrals are even more valuable, as guests are more likely to book a property based on the recommendations of people who have already stayed there. In this chapter, we will explore some innovative techniques to supercharge your guest referral game and take your business to the next level.

1. Create a Referral Program: One of the most straightforward ways to encourage guests to refer their friends and family is to create a referral program. Offer incentives like discounts, free stays, or gift cards to guests who refer others to your property.
2. Personalized Thank You Cards: Personalized thank you cards are a great way to show your guests how much you appreciate their business. Include a handwritten note thanking them for their stay and encouraging them to refer their friends and family.
3. Social Media Shoutouts: Use your social media accounts to shout out guests who have referred others to your property. Make sure to tag them and thank them publicly for their support.
4. Highlight Referral Success Stories: Share success stories of guests who have referred others to your property. This can be done through blog posts, social media, or email newsletters.
5. Offer an Exclusive Referral Discount: Offer a special discount or promotion exclusively for guests who refer others to your property. This not only incentivizes referrals but also rewards loyal guests.

6. Host Referral Contests: Host a referral contest where guests can win prizes for referring the most people to your property. This can be a great way to generate buzz and excitement around your business.
7. Partner with Local Businesses: Partner with local businesses to offer joint promotions or referral programs. For example, team up with a local restaurant to offer guests a discount at your property if they dine at the restaurant.
8. Utilize Guest Surveys: Use guest surveys to ask about their experience and if they would refer others to your property. If they indicate they would, follow up with a personalized thank you and referral incentive.
9. Offer Referral Incentives to Past Guests: Reach out to past guests and offer them a referral incentive to refer others to your property. This can be a great way to reactivate past guests and generate new business.
10. Leverage Email Marketing: Use email marketing to promote your referral program and offer incentives to guests who refer others. Make sure to segment your email list to target guests who are most likely to refer others.
11. Create a Referral Landing Page: Create a dedicated landing page on your website that explains your referral program and highlights the benefits of referring others to your property.
12. Create Referral Graphics: Create social media graphics or email templates that guests can easily share with their friends and family. Make it easy for them to refer others to your property.
13. Highlight Your Referral Program in Your Property Listings: Make sure to highlight your referral program in your property listings on sites like VRBO and Airbnb. This can be a great way to attract guests who are looking for referral incentives.
14. Use Influencer Marketing: Partner with influencers in your niche to promote your property and referral program to their followers. This can be a great way to reach a new audience and generate referrals.
15. Follow Up with Referrals: Make sure to follow up with guests who have been referred to your property. Reach out to them personally and offer them an incentive to book their stay.

Referrals are a powerful tool for growing your vacation rental business. By implementing these innovative techniques, you can supercharge your referral game and take your vacation business to the next level of success.

The psychology behind word-of-mouth vacation rental marketing

According to a study conducted by Nielsen, 92% of consumers trust recommendations from friends and family over all other forms of advertising. This means that getting guests to talk positively about your vacation rental property can have a significant impact on your business.

But what makes someone want to refer your property to others?

One reason is the feeling of social currency. People want to feel good about themselves, and by referring to a great vacation rental property, they can elevate their own status among their friends and family. Additionally, people often like to help others, and referring to a great vacation rental property is a way to do just that.

Another important factor is the emotional connection guests have with your property. According to a study by Harris Interactive, emotional connection can drive twice as much word-of-mouth as customer satisfaction alone.

This means that guests who have an emotional connection to your property are more likely to talk about it with others and refer it to friends and family.

So how do you create an emotional connection with your guests? One way is through personalization. By making your guests feel valued and special, you can create a bond that will make them want to refer your property to others.

Personalization can come in many forms, such as welcome notes, personalized recommendations for local attractions, or even just remembering their names.

Another way to create an emotional connection is through storytelling. People love a good story, and if you can tell the story of your property in a compelling way, you can create an emotional connection with your guests.

Share the history of your property, highlight its unique features, and tell the story of how it came to be a vacation rental. This will not only create an emotional connection with your guests, but it will also give them a story to share with others.

Finally, creating an emotional connection with your guests requires excellent customer service. According to a study by American Express, 70% of Americans are willing to spend an average of 13% more with companies that provide excellent customer service.

By providing exceptional customer service, you can create a positive emotional connection with your guests that will make them want to refer your property to others.

In conclusion, understanding the psychology behind word-of-mouth marketing is crucial to getting guests talking about your vacation rental property.

By creating an emotional connection with your guests through personalization, storytelling, and excellent customer service, you can supercharge your referral game and take your business to the next level.

THIRTEEN:
The Science of Comfort:
How Temperature Affects Your Vacation Rental

As a vacation rental owner, one of the most important factors in providing your guests with a comfortable and enjoyable stay is the temperature of the rental. It might seem like a minor detail, but studies have shown that the temperature of a space can have a significant impact on the overall experience of the guest.

To begin, let's look at the science behind temperature and its effects on human comfort. The human body is designed to maintain a relatively constant internal temperature of around 98.6°F (37°C).

When the temperature around us changes, our body works to regulate its internal temperature through a process called thermoregulation. This process involves the dilation or constriction of blood vessels in the skin, sweating, and shivering, among other responses.

As a vacation rental owner, you know that your guests' comfort is paramount to a positive experience. And when it comes to comfort, temperature plays a critical role. Not only does the temperature set the tone for the overall experience, but it can also affect mood, sleep, and even cognitive function.

The Science Behind Temperature and Comfort

To understand the impact of temperature on comfort, it's important to understand the basics of thermoregulation, and the body's ability to regulate its internal temperature. The human body is designed to maintain a core temperature of around 98.6 degrees Fahrenheit, and it does so through a process called homeostasis.

When the body's internal temperature rises above or falls below this range, the body reacts by initiating mechanisms to restore the temperature to the normal range.

Research has shown that the ideal temperature range for comfort is between 68 and 72 degrees Fahrenheit. Within this range, the body doesn't have to work as hard to maintain its core temperature, and guests are less likely to feel too hot or too cold.

However, it's important to note that individual preferences can vary, and guests may have different temperature preferences depending on factors such as age, gender, and activity level.

The Importance of Airflow

While temperature is a critical factor in comfort, airflow is also important. Stagnant air can make guests feel uncomfortable and can also contribute to poor air quality. This is particularly important in areas with high humidity, where stagnant air can lead to mold growth and other issues.

One way to improve airflow is to use ceiling fans or portable fans. Fans help to circulate the air and can make guests feel cooler even if the temperature is slightly higher than their preferred range. Fans are also a good option in areas where AC is not plumbed into an existing unit.

When the temperature is too hot or too cold, it can cause discomfort and even lead to health problems. Heat exhaustion, heatstroke, and hypothermia are all serious conditions that can arise from exposure to extreme temperatures.

While the temperatures found in vacation rentals are unlikely to cause such severe issues, they can still have a significant impact on the comfort and well-being of your guests. It's best to stage the rooms, and set a comfortable and affordable setting for the guests upon every arrival.

One factor to consider is humidity. High humidity can make the air feel warmer, while low humidity can make it feel cooler. In humid climates, it may be necessary to lower the temperature to maintain a comfortable environment. Conversely, in dry climates, raising the temperature slightly may help prevent dryness and discomfort.

Another important factor is air circulation. Stagnant air can cause discomfort, particularly in warmer temperatures. It's essential to ensure that there is adequate air circulation in the rental, whether through the use of fans, open windows, or air conditioning.

Speaking of air conditioning, it's worth noting that this can be a particularly effective way to regulate the temperature in a vacation rental. However, it's important to use it wisely. Using the air conditioning excessively can lead to high energy bills and can be harmful to the environment. Encourage your guests to use the air conditioning only when necessary and to turn it off when they leave the rental.

There are also some other tips that can help maintain a comfortable temperature in your vacation rental. For example, using blackout curtains or shades can help to keep the rental cool in the summer by blocking out the sun's heat. In the winter, using thicker curtains or window insulation film can help to keep the rental warm by preventing heat from escaping through the windows.

In conclusion, the temperature of your vacation rental is a crucial factor in ensuring your guests have a comfortable and enjoyable stay.

By understanding the science behind temperature regulation and taking steps to maintain a comfortable environment, you can provide your guests with a 5-star experience that will keep them coming back year after year.

Staging Portable AC Units

In areas where central air conditioning is not available, portable AC units can be a good option for keeping guests cool and comfortable. However, it's important to stage the units properly to ensure optimal performance.

One key factor to consider is the placement of the unit. Portable AC units should be placed in areas where they can draw in the fresh air and expel hot air. This means that the unit should be placed near a window or other opening, and the exhaust hose should be properly vented to the outside.

Another factor to consider is the size of the unit. Portable AC units come in a range of sizes, and it's important to choose a unit that is appropriately sized for the space. A unit that is too small will struggle to cool the space, while a unit that is too large will cycle on and off frequently, which can lead to poor performance and increased energy costs.

Conclusion

When it comes to creating a comfortable environment for your guests, temperature, and airflow are critical factors.

By understanding the science behind temperature and comfort and using portable AC units and fans as needed, you can ensure that your guests have a pleasant and comfortable stay.

With a little attention to detail, you can create a 5-star experience that will keep your guests coming back year after year.

FOURTEEN:
Mastering the Art of Buying a Vacation Rental for Maximum Profit

Evaluating the Market

Before investing in a vacation rental property, it's essential to evaluate the market to ensure that your investment will be profitable. This section will discuss key considerations for evaluating the market, including location, local tourism industry, and competition."

The location of a vacation rental property is one of the most critical factors to consider when evaluating the market. A prime location will attract more guests, resulting in higher occupancy rates and rental income.

Some key factors to consider when evaluating the location of a potential vacation rental property include proximity to tourist attractions, beaches, restaurants, and shopping centers.

It's also important to consider the local tourism industry. Researching local tourism statistics, including visitor numbers and revenue, can provide insights into the potential profitability of your investment.

Additionally, understanding the seasonality of the local tourism industry is important, as it will impact the number of guests and rates that can be charged. For example, if the area experiences a significant slowdown in the off-season, it may be necessary to adjust the rates or offer specials to maintain occupancy.

Another important factor to consider when evaluating the market is competition. It's essential to research other vacation rental properties in the area to determine the level of competition and what sets your property apart from others.

One way to do this is by looking at online booking platforms and reviewing the rates, amenities, and guest reviews of competing properties.

Additionally, it's crucial to research any regulations or restrictions that may impact your vacation rental property's profitability. For example, some municipalities may have specific zoning laws or rental regulations that could impact your ability to rent out your property on a short-term basis.

Understanding the market is critical when making a decision about investing in a vacation rental property. By carefully evaluating the location, local tourism industry, competition, and any relevant regulations or restrictions, investors can make informed decisions about their investment and maximize their potential return on investment.

Research shows that vacation rental properties can provide higher returns on investment than traditional long-term rental properties. However, these returns depend on the property's location, demand, and management.

By evaluating the market carefully, investors can ensure that their vacation rental property is a profitable and worthwhile investment.

Assessing Your Expenses and Profitability

When investing in a vacation rental property, it's crucial to assess your expenses and profitability. Understanding these factors is essential for making informed decisions and maximizing your return on investment.

One of the first expenses to consider is the cost of purchasing the property. This includes not only the purchase price but also any closing costs, legal fees, and property inspections. Additionally, you'll need to factor in ongoing expenses such as property taxes, insurance, maintenance, and repairs.

To calculate your profitability, you'll need to analyze the expected income from renting out your property. This includes not only rental income but also any additional income from amenities or services such as cleaning fees, late checkout fees, or concierge services.

When estimating your income, it's important to consider the seasonality of the market and the demand for your property. This will impact your rental rates and your overall occupancy rate.

To calculate your profitability, subtract your total expenses from your expected income. This will give you an estimate of your net income, which is a crucial factor in assessing the profitability of your vacation rental property.

It's important to note that profitability is not the only factor to consider when investing in a vacation rental property. Other factors, such as the location and condition of the property, can also impact your investment.

In addition, it's important to have a contingency plan in case of unexpected expenses or periods of low occupancy. This can include having a reserve fund or considering alternative uses for the property such as long-term rentals or even selling the property if necessary.

By carefully assessing your expenses and profitability, you can make informed decisions and ensure that your investment in a vacation rental property is financially sound."

Property Selection

Once you've determined the market and financing options, it's time to start looking at potential properties. Selecting the right vacation rental property is crucial for long-term profitability. Here are some key considerations to keep in mind:

1. Location: The location of the property is the single most important factor to consider. The ideal location will depend on the type of vacation rental property you're looking for. For example, if you're targeting families, look for a property near family-friendly attractions. If you're targeting couples or retirees, look for a property in a quiet, peaceful location.

2. Property Type: The type of vacation rental property you choose will also impact your profitability. There are several types of vacation rental properties, including condos, townhouses, single-family homes, and villas. Each type of property has its own advantages and disadvantages. For example, condos and townhouses are often less expensive to purchase and maintain, while single-family homes and villas offer more space and privacy.

3. Property Size: The size of the property is another important consideration. You'll want to choose a property that's large enough to accommodate your target audience, but not so large that it's difficult to maintain. Consider factors such as the number of bedrooms and bathrooms, as well as the size of the living spaces.

4. Amenities: The amenities you offer can make or break your vacation rental property. Consider what amenities your target audience is looking for, such as a pool, hot tub, or beach access. However, be mindful of the cost of these amenities, as they can significantly impact your profitability.

5. Condition: The condition of the property is also an important factor to consider. Make sure to thoroughly inspect the property before making an offer, and consider the cost of any repairs or upgrades that may be necessary.

6. Management and Maintenance: Finally, consider the management and maintenance of the property. Will you manage the property yourself or hire a property management company? What are the costs associated with maintenance and repairs? These factors can significantly impact your long-term profitability.

By carefully considering these factors, you can select the right vacation rental property for long-term profitability.

Property Management - Preemptive Research

As a vacation rental property owner, finding the right property manager is critical to the success of your investment. It's important to take your time and carefully evaluate your options to ensure that you choose a property manager who will help you achieve your goals.

One of the first steps in selecting a property manager is to do your research. Start by researching property management companies in the area where you plan to purchase a vacation rental property. Look for companies with a good reputation, positive reviews, and experience managing properties similar to yours.

When you have a list of potential property management companies, start reaching out to them to gather more information. Ask for references from current and past clients, and ask about their experience managing vacation rental properties.

You should also ask about their marketing strategy, how they handle bookings and reservations, and how they handle guest complaints.

Once you've narrowed down your list of potential property managers, it's time to schedule an in-person meeting. This will give you a chance to meet with the property manager, ask questions, and get a sense of their overall approach to managing vacation rental properties.

During the meeting, be sure to ask about their fees and any additional charges you may incur. You should also ask about their insurance coverage and any liability issues you may need to be aware of. If you're unsure about any aspect of the property manager's services, don't be afraid to ask for clarification.

When you've chosen a property manager, be sure to sign a contract that outlines all the terms of your agreement. This should include details about the manager's fees, how often they will communicate with you, and what services they will provide.

In addition to finding the right property manager, there are a few other things you can do to ensure the long-term profitability of your vacation rental property.

These include:

- Keeping your property in good condition: Regular maintenance and repairs are essential for keeping your property in good condition and preventing costly problems down the line.

- Staying up to date with local regulations: Laws and regulations related to vacation rental properties can vary widely by location. Stay informed about any changes to local laws and regulations that may impact your investment.

- Maintaining a positive relationship with your guests: Happy guests are more likely to return to your property and recommend it to others. Make sure your guests feel welcome and comfortable during their stay.

By following these tips and taking the time to carefully select a property manager, you can maximize the profitability of your vacation rental property and enjoy a successful investment.

Maintaining and Upgrading the Property

Investing in a vacation rental property isn't just about buying it, but also about maintaining and upgrading it to keep it profitable in the long run. In this section, we'll discuss some key considerations for maintaining and upgrading a vacation rental property.

1. Preemptive Upgrades: It's important to consider the upgrades that may be necessary before purchasing a vacation rental property. This will give you an idea of the potential costs and difficulties involved in upgrading the property. Some things to consider are the age and condition of the property, the availability of contractors and suppliers in the area, and any local regulations that may affect your ability to make upgrades.

2. Property Assessment: Before making any upgrades, it's important to assess the property and identify areas that need improvement. This could include anything from outdated appliances to damaged floors or walls. Once you have a clear idea of what needs to be addressed, you can begin to develop a plan for upgrading the property.

3. Local Market: Upgrading a vacation rental property can be a challenge, particularly in areas with limited availability of contractors or suppliers. It's important to research the local market and identify potential challenges you may face when making upgrades. This could include issues with shipping or obtaining certain materials, or a lack of qualified contractors in the area.

4. Budgeting: When upgrading a vacation rental property, it's important to set a realistic budget and stick to it. This will help you avoid overspending and ensure that you are able to generate a profit from your investment. You should also consider the potential return on investment for any upgrades you make, and focus on those that will have the most impact on the property's profitability.

5. Maintenance: In addition to upgrading the property, it's important to maintain it to keep it in good condition and ensure that guests have a comfortable and enjoyable stay. This could include regular cleaning, repairs, and upkeep of the property's systems and appliances.

By considering these factors when maintaining and upgrading your vacation rental property, you can ensure that it remains profitable for years to come.

Lynn's Top 25 Checklist For Success:

Investing in a vacation rental property can be a profitable and rewarding experience, but it requires careful planning, research, and execution.

By evaluating the market, selecting the right property, screening and hiring property managers, and maintaining and upgrading the property, you can maximize your investment and ensure long-term profitability.

1. Evaluate the local tourism industry and the competition in the area.
2. Determine the most desirable location based on rental demand and market trends.
3. Consider the costs of purchasing a vacation rental property and calculate your potential ROI.
4. Research local regulations and tax laws to avoid any legal issues.
5. Evaluate the property for its potential rental income and make sure it meets your budget and investment goals.
6. Research and select the right mortgage lender.

7. Hire a reputable home inspector to check the property's condition.
8. Hire a real estate attorney to review the contract and protect your interests.
9. Develop a marketing plan to attract renters and maximize rental income.
10. Create a rental agreement that covers all the necessary terms and conditions.
11. Set a fair rental rate based on the local market.
12. Screen potential renters to minimize the risk of property damage or loss.
13. Develop a checklist for cleaning and maintenance between renters.
14. Hire a reliable property manager to handle maintenance and repairs.
15. Consider using property management software to streamline communication and record-keeping.
16. Develop an emergency response plan in case of property damage or natural disasters.
17. Upgrade and maintain the property regularly to ensure renters are satisfied.
18. Develop a guest experience plan to enhance your renters' experience and leave a lasting impression.
19. Stay up-to-date on local market trends and adjust your marketing and rental rates accordingly.
20. Develop a system for responding to renters' complaints and concerns promptly.
21. Keep accurate financial records and consult with a tax professional to optimize your deductions.
22. Invest in a homeowner's insurance policy and renter's insurance, to protect your investment.
23. Consider incorporating your rental property as an LLC or corporation to limit your liability.
24. Keep track of maintenance expenses to avoid overspending on unnecessary repairs.
25. Stay organized and proactive to maximize your rental income and ensure long-term profitability.

Remember, the key to success is to remain proactive and informed every step of the way and always follow a checklist for success.

FIFTEEN:
Resources for Success: Your Guide to Becoming a Vacation Rental Pro

Lynn's Recommended Reading List

Here are 20 books on the subject of vacation rental ownership, listed in order of my most recommended reads:

1. "The Airbnb Story" by Leigh Gallagher
2. "The Vacation Rental Blueprint" by Erica Muller
3. "How to Make Money on Airbnb" by Sally Miller
4. "Vacation Rental Success: Insider Secrets to Profitably Own, Market, and Manage Vacation Rental Property" by Joel Rasmussen
5. "The Business of Airbnb: How I Made Six Figures in 18 Months" by Brett Tharp
6. "The Vacation Rental Goldmine: How to Maximize Your Rental Income With Great Guest Experiences" by Chris DeBusk
7. "Get Paid for Your Pad" by Jasper Ribbers
8. "The Airbnb Entrepreneur" by Patrick Astre
9. "Vacation Rental Owner's Manual: Vacation Rental Success Blueprint" by Dave Reina
10. "Profitable Airbnb Listing: How to Maximize Your Rental Income, Boost Your Bookings, and Stand Out in the Crowd" by Laura Otero
11. "Short-Term Rental Success Stories from the Edge" by Richard Fertig
12. "How to Make Money on Vacation Rentals: Even Without Owning a Property" by James Klobasa
13. "Airbnb Hosting Guide: The Ultimate Collection of Airbnb Hosting Tips and Tricks" by Alex Wong
14. "The Airbnb Expert's Playbook: Secrets to Making Six-Figures as a Rentalpreneur" by Aaron Zadek
15. "The Short Term Rental Playbook: For Rental Income and Early Retirement" by Alex Wong
16. "The Airbnb Superhost Checklist: How to Maximize Your Earnings as a Host" by Nathan Rice
17. "The Vacation Rental Owners Handbook: The Essential Guide to Success and Profit" by Debbie Elicksen
18. "Airbnb Income: How to Make Money with Airbnb" by Josephine Smith
19. "The Airbnb Profit Blueprint: Learn How I Made $5000+ a Month with Airbnb" by Pamela Russell

20. "Vacation Rental Marketing Secrets: The Simple Guide to Generating More Bookings" by Tracey Woodcock.

These books offer valuable insights and strategies for anyone interested in buying and managing a vacation rental property. They cover a wide range of topics, from market research and property selection to property management and marketing.

Podcasts and YouTube Channels

Another great resource for vacation rental owners are podcasts and YouTube channels. Here are 10 on my recommended list:

1. Vacation Rental Success by Heather Bayer
2. The Vacation Rental Show by Matt Landau
3. STR Profit Academy by Richard Fertig
4. The STR Revenue Podcast by Antonio Bortolotti
5. Hostfully Hospitality Podcast by Margot Schmorak
6. Get Paid For Your Pad by Jasper Ribbers
7. The Short-Term Shop by Angie Slone
8. Short-Term Rental Secrets by Julie George
9. Boostly by Mark Simpson
10. Vacation Rental Machine by Seth Williams

Each of these podcasts and YouTube channels offers unique perspectives, tips, and insights on owning and managing a vacation rental property.

From marketing strategies to guest communication, these resources cover it all.

Lenders To Consider

Here's the list of mortgage companies, lenders or banks that could be beneficial to vacation rental owners along with some of their known advantages.

1. Quicken Loans: Provides quick and easy online mortgage applications for vacation rental properties.
2. Wells Fargo: Offers vacation rental property loans with low down payments and competitive interest rates.
3. US Bank: Provides financing options for vacation rental properties in popular tourist destinations.
4. Bank of America: Offers vacation rental property loans with flexible terms and competitive interest rates.
5. SoFi: Provides vacation rental property loans with no hidden fees or prepayment penalties.
6. Chase: Offers financing options for vacation rental properties with competitive interest rates.
7. Ally Bank: Provides vacation rental property loans with low down payments and flexible repayment terms.

8. Rocket Mortgage: Offers vacation rental property loans with fast and easy online applications.
9. PNC Bank: Provides vacation rental property loans with competitive interest rates and flexible repayment terms.
10. BB&T: Offers financing options for vacation rental properties in popular tourist destinations.
11. SunTrust Bank: Provides vacation rental property loans with low down payments and competitive interest rates.
12. First Internet Bank: Offers vacation rental property loans with low closing costs and competitive interest rates.
13. TD Bank: Provides financing options for vacation rental properties with competitive interest rates and flexible repayment terms.
14. Discover Home Loans: Offers vacation rental property loans with no origination fees and flexible repayment terms.
15. Flagstar Bank: Provides vacation rental property loans with competitive interest rates and low closing costs.
16. Fulton Bank: Offers financing options for vacation rental properties with flexible repayment terms.
17. HomeBridge Financial Services: Provides vacation rental property loans with competitive interest rates and low down payments.
18. HSBC: Offers vacation rental property loans with flexible repayment terms and competitive interest rates.
19. PrimeLending: Provides financing options for vacation rental properties in popular tourist destinations.
20. U.S. Mortgage of Florida: Offers vacation rental property loans with low down payments and competitive interest rates.

These are some of the mortgage companies, lenders, or banks that could provide financing options for vacation rental properties. However, it is important to note that policies and rates can vary based on location, property type, and borrower qualifications. It is recommended to shop around and compare offers from multiple lenders to find the best deal.

Conclusion

Running a successful vacation rental business is both an art and a science. It takes a deep understanding of your guests, your competition, and the broader industry landscape to truly stand out and thrive.

After reading this book, you should have a much better understanding of what it takes to be a successful vacation rental property owner. From evaluating the market and selecting the right property to upgrading and maintaining it, we've covered all the necessary steps to maximize your investment and minimize your stress.

Throughout this book, we've explored a range of strategies, techniques, and insights that can help you achieve that success. From mastering the art of storytelling to embracing the power of technology, from building a rock-solid brand to tapping into the psychology of referrals, we've covered a lot of ground.

One key takeaway from this book is the importance of attention to detail. Whether it's maintaining a comfortable temperature, selecting the right property, or managing your rental, every detail counts when it comes to guest satisfaction and long-term profitability.

Additionally, we've explored the benefits of using property management companies and the resources available to help you succeed, such as books, podcasts, and mortgage lenders.

But remember, this is just the beginning. The vacation rental market is constantly evolving, and it's essential to stay up-to-date with the latest trends and best practices. Continue to educate yourself, network with other property owners, and stay open to new ideas and opportunities.

Ultimately, being a successful vacation rental property owner requires hard work, dedication, and a passion for providing exceptional guest experiences. By following the advice and insights in this book, you'll be well on your way to achieving your goals and realizing your dreams as a vacation rental property owner.

But at the end of the day, the most important ingredient in your success is you. Your passion, your creativity, your persistence. Your ability to connect with guests on a deep, emotional level and create experiences that they'll never forget.

So go out there and make it happen. Take everything you've learned here and put it into action. Embrace the challenges, learn from your mistakes, and always keep your guests at the center of everything you do.

Remember, your vacation rental business is not just a way to make a living. It's a way to make a difference in the lives of your guests. To create memories that will last a lifetime. To share your passion for travel, adventure, and hospitality with the world.

So go out there and make it happen. We believe in you, and we're excited to see what you'll achieve.